more!
hand appliqué by machine

9 QUILT PROJECTS | UPDATED TECHNIQUES | NEEDLE-TURN RESULTS WITHOUT HANDWORK

Beth Ferrier

C&T PUBLISHING

Text copyright © 2009 by Beth Ferrier

Artwork copyright © 2009 by C&T Publishing, Inc.

Publisher: Amy Marson

Creative Director: Gailen Runge

Acquisitions Editor: Susanne Woods

Editor: Cynthia Bix

Technical Editors: Ann Haley and Sandy Peterson

Copyeditor and Proofreader: Wordfirm Inc.

Cover/Book Designer: Kristen Yenche

Production Coordinator: Zinnia Heinzmann

Production Editor: Julia Cianci

Illustrator: Beth Ferrier

Photography by Christina Carty-Francis and **Diane Pedersen** of C&T Publishing, Inc., unless otherwise noted.

Published by C&T Publishing, Inc., P.O. Box 1456, Lafayette, CA 94549

Library of Congress Cataloging-in-Publication Data

Ferrier, Beth.

More! hand appliqué by machine : 9 quilt projects, updated techniques, needle-turn results without handwork / by Beth Ferrier.

p. cm.

ISBN 978-1-57120-832-3 (soft cover)

1. Machine appliqué--Patterns. 2. Patchwork. 3. Quilting. I. Title.

TT779.F47 2009

746.44'5042--dc22

2009012927

Printed in China

10 9 8 7 6 5 4 3 2 1

dedication

To Kent—you believed in me even when I didn't— for that I will love you forever.

acknowledgments

My previous books were all self-published, making me, for better or worse, the boss of everything. Working with the lovely folks at C&T—especially my editor, Cynthia Bix—has made writing this book a joy.

Many thanks to Patti Carey at Northcott Silk Inc. and Anna Fishkin at Red Rooster Fabrics for their generosity in providing fabric for samples. Thanks also to Heather and Bob Purcell at Superior Threads, Barb Douglas at Presencia Threads, and Nancy Storch at WonderFil Threads. They've all kept this fabric and thread junkie well supplied.

And as always, thanks to my family. To Kent, for bringing home dinners, and to Karen Boutté, my best friend forever, for hauling me in off the ledge.

contents

introduction

When I was first learning to quilt, I despaired that beautiful appliqué was only the work of needle-turn goddesses. Being the stubborn sort (though I prefer to think of myself as tenacious), I set out to conquer appliqué.

Because I'm almost pathologically curious and willing to experiment, I spent the next few years trying all sorts of appliqué techniques. I found myself wondering why it seemed that we quilters were so often doing things the hard way. Bit by bit I kept the parts of a technique that I liked and searched for better options to replace those I didn't. It took the chiding of my students to finally understand that I had, indeed, come up with a new approach to appliqué, one that I needed to write down.

The result was my first book, *Hand Appliqué by Machine.* In the years since that first book was published, the quilting industry has blessed us with fantastic new products, making traditional techniques easier to achieve and allowing us to take our appliqué in nifty new directions.

My goal has always been to find a way to make appliqué fun and easy without sacrificing that turned edge. But most of all, I wanted to make appliqué free-spirited again—open to interpretation instead of persnickety perfection. So come on, grab your scissors, and let's play!

#### CHAPTER ONE

the basics

W e've got to walk before we can run, or so they say. So let's saunter down memory lane with an overview of the basic hand appliqué by machine technique that I introduced in my first book. While the essence of the original technique is unchanged, I have fine-tuned it a bit over the years. If this is your first stroll along this path, not to worry, I'll have you up to speed in no time. (I promise, that's the last of the pedestrian puns.)

In a nutshell, this technique takes the old "freezer paper, gluestick, invisible thread, and blind hem stitch" method and turns it on its head. Instead of starting with the background and building up, we're going to complete our appliqués before stitching them down. We'll learn how to fine-tune our machines so that our stitches completely disappear. (It's so much fun to have people insist that our appliqué couldn't possibly have been done by machine.) And this is all done with a process that is so fun, forgiving, and fast that we just might have time to make all the quilts we want after all!

In the chapters to follow, you'll see just how versatile and creative this technique can be.

getting started

No matter what method is used for appliqué, it's the prep work that takes the most time. The following steps are designed to reduce the time spent getting ready to appliqué—without sacrificing any of the quality.

Having spent so much of my life in Michigan, I've acquired an appreciation for the efficiency of assembly lines. So, we're going to set up our own little appliqué assembly line.

GATHER YOUR SUPPLIES

Here's what you need:

• Freezer paper

 tip

Grocery store freezer paper is just fine. However, freezer paper sheets made especially for quilters are often sturdier and adhere better, making them worth the price. *Plus* the sheets are already cut to the perfect size for running through an inkjet printer. Try Quilter's Freezer Paper Sheets or Ricky Tims' Extra-Wide Freezer Paper, both available from C&T Publishing (see Resources, page 80).

• Scissors (one pair of dressmaker and one 4″ or 5″ pair)

• Stapler and staple remover

• Gluestick (My current favorite is Avery Dennison, which is available from office supply stores.)

• Long cuticle stick

• Inkjet printer (optional)

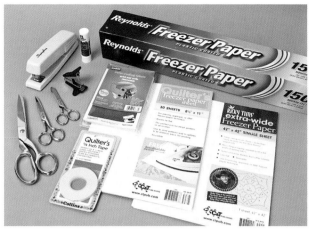

Tools and materials

- Invisible thread (Superior or Sulky polyester; all other brands are nylon, which does not work as well)
- 50-weight cotton thread in a neutral color for the bobbin
- 70/10 sharps sewing machine needles

Needles and threads

- Sewing machine with adjustable stitch width and length
- Open-toe or clear plastic foot

Machine with open-toe foot

start with the leaves

The project that I designed to illustrate the basics of hand appliqué by machine is *Ring O' Posies*. (See page 38 for the specific fabric requirements, directions, and templates for this wallhanging.)

To complete the project exactly as I did, you'll need ten leaves, six flowers, and thirteen berries. Now, we could trace the design onto template plastic, cut it out using our worst scissors (because we wouldn't want to wreck our best pair), trace ten leaves onto freezer paper, and then cut them all out individually. Golly-gosh, doesn't that sound like fun? I didn't think so, either.

Instead, make a couple photocopies of the *Ring O' Posies* templates (page 41). You'll use one photocopy to make your templates and one to keep as a key so you don't mess up your pretty new book.

Write "Key" on the top of one of the photocopies, and set it aside. Loosely cut the appliqué templates out of the other photocopy. (Just chunk them out for now.)

Label one photocopy "Key."

ONTO THE FREEZER PAPER

You'll want to make the nicest freezer paper templates possible. Their quality determines how easily the rest of the appliqué process happens.

To make a lot of leaves in a little time, we can fold or stack the freezer paper until we have six layers, which is the magic number of layers that can be cut accurately.

Rip out about a 1-yard length of freezer paper. Then fold it in half lengthwise, plastic sides together. Now accordion fold it twice so that the ragged torn edges extend past the folds. Crease the paper well; if needed, put a staple in each corner to hold the stack flat.

CUE THE STAPLER

Now rustle up those leaf templates, and staple them to the freezer paper. Each leaf needs a couple of staples, one toward the point and one at the round end. Keep the staples inside the lines—we'll be cutting on those lines.

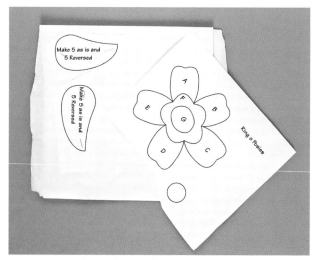

Staple templates to freezer paper sandwich.

Because the freezer paper templates are so important, rough cut the stack first, just separating each complete motif for now.

Templates stapled and rough cut

LET THE CUTTING BEGIN

Believe it or not, I use my very best dressmaker scissors to cut out my freezer paper shapes. To create the best possible templates, I need my strongest (so I can cut through seven layers of paper), sharpest (so the edges aren't all smashed together), most accurate pair of scissors, and that would be my 8-inch Gingher scissors. Not only are they excellent scissors that hold their edge well, but they can also be sent back to the company for repair and sharpening for a very small fee. These are my forever scissors. (And no, I'm not on the dole with Gingher; I'm just a happy customer.)

> ❋ **tip**
>
> It's not true that paper dulls scissors; rock dulls scissors, paper covers rock. (Work with me here.) It's actually the coating on the paper that dulls the scissors. Keep the scissors clean (I just wipe them on my jeans!) and you'll be able to use your marvelous scissors on both fabric and paper.

Cut out leaf templates, cutting through all freezer paper layers, more or less on the line. Because of the way these shapes will be organized, we don't have to be perfectly exact when we cut them apart. What's most important is that the cuts are smooth so that the turned edges can be free of the dreaded "pokies."

I cut over a waste can to catch the paper scraps. Once you are done cutting, set the remainder of the freezer paper stack aside for the rest of the project.

Trim templates.

TA-DA! YOU'VE GOT TEMPLATES

A staple remover will make short work of pulling the staples from the leaves. Toss away the photocopy layer.

 tip

If you're using your home scanner and an inkjet printer, you can print those first copies directly onto freezer paper. But don't just print out a page of leaves! Who wants to cut them each individually anyway? Also, *never* feed any type of freezer paper into a photocopy machine or a laser printer. The heat will melt the plastic side and seize up the printer.

So, in just a few minutes, we have twelve leaf perfect templates, half of them mirror images. We achieved that by the clever way we accordion-folded or stacked the freezer paper.

AND NOW TO THE FABRIC

Set your iron to scorch. (That would be the cotton/linen setting.) Place the selected fabrics *wrong side up* on the ironing board. The shiny side of the templates goes face down on the fabric. Press each template with that hot iron to create a temporary bond.

Leave at least an inch between the paper templates, as we'll be adding seam allowances when we cut out the shapes. Now, roughly cut the shapes out of the fabric.

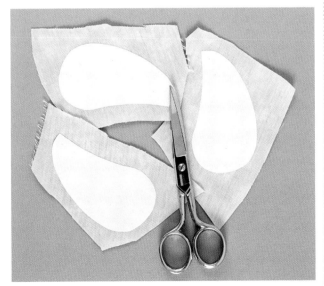
Rough cut fabric around templates.

It's nice to have tidy seam allowances. It really does make a difference in the look of the final project. Next, carefully cut around each template as you add the seam allowance. Shoot for a scant ¼" seam allowance to start. More complex shapes may require a smaller seam allowance, but smaller is harder to turn.

 tip

Use quilter's ¼" tape on your nondominant thumb as a guide for the seam allowance. You don't have to measure every bit; just use it as a reference until you get the hang of it.

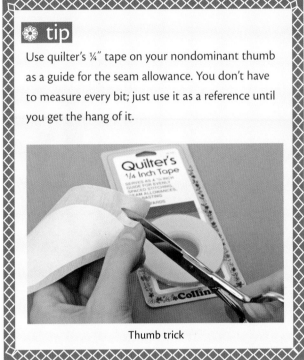
Thumb trick

MITER THE POINTS

There's a lot of extra seam allowance sticking out from the point, which will create unpleasant bulk if you leave it. I simply snip it away, straight across the point, leaving about a ⅛" seam allowance. I call this mitering the points.

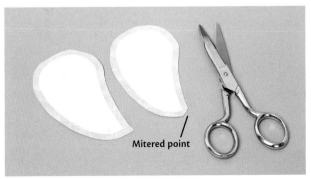
Mitered point

Right point is snipped, or mitered.

DANGEROUS CURVES AHEAD

Finally, cut a couple tiny clips in the little dip on the leaf. Only inside curves need to be clipped; clipping outside curves can result in a nasty case of the "pokies." Clip to just within a few threads of the paper. Clipping all the way to the paper, especially in tight spaces, can result in hairy pokies—quite unsightly.

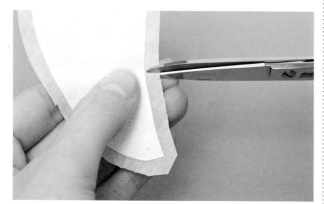

Clip curves.

THE PERFECT GLUESTICK

What we want is a gluestick that is tacky enough to catch on the first pinch and moist enough to give us time to adjust the seam allowances.

Pretty much any brand of gluestick will do. Somewhere on the package you need to find the words "washes out" or "water soluble" or even "nontoxic." I really like the Avery Dennison brand the best. Elmer's is good, and UHU is also excellent.

Some folks love to use liquid glues, like school glues that come in bottles, but for me, that type is just too wet. It takes too long to dry enough to turn the seam allowance.

Avery Dennison also makes a wonderful glue pen, exactly ¼" in diameter, that is perfect for glue basting. The downside is that glue pens are a lot more expensive. I keep a couple in my appliqué kit for working on teeny tiny stuff.

THE FINE POINTS OF GLUE BASTING

Keep the glue on the fabric seam allowance only. Glue on the paper equals glue on the fingers. That's pretty much it.

Let's get back to those leaves. Apply the gluestick to the trimmed-off seam allowance at the point. Carefully fold over the seam allowance, sticking it to the freezer paper and being very careful to avoid bending the freezer paper point. Now apply the glue to the remaining exposed fabric seam allowance and the folded-over part. Working clockwise around the shape, pinch the seam allowance to the freezer paper. You'll be able to feel the edge of the template as the guide. Be gentle—it's only paper.

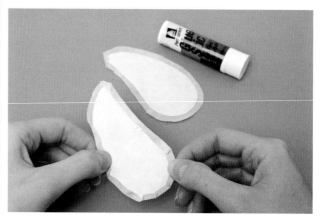

Pinch seam all around.

THE MAGIC WAND

Okay, so for most folks, it's just a cuticle stick. But when you see how you can use this stick to pet those pokies right away from the edges, you'll think it's magic, too. One of the cool things about using glue for basting is that you never have to settle for less than the best when it comes to the turned edge. Pet, poke, prod, lift, and re-glue as needed until the leaf is a thing of beauty. Repeat nine more times to create enough leaves for *Ring O' Posies*.

Use the "magic wand" to finesse the seam allowances.

GOING IN CIRCLES

In the appliqué universe, perfect circles are a way of showing off. But we can achieve them simply by using adhesive office dot labels instead of making freezer paper templates. These dots, which can be found in office supply stores, are used in filing systems and come in a variety of sizes. Because I'm appliqué addicted, I own some of every size. The *Ring O' Posies* project uses ¾" dots.

Sometimes the adhesive on the dots is a little too strong, making it hard to remove when we're done. To solve that, before sticking them to the wrong side of the fabric, simply touch the dots to fabric to lint up the adhesive a bit. To adhere them to our desired fabrics, no iron is needed—just press them into place with your fingers.

Trim the seam allowances at about ³⁄₁₆" or a *scant* quarter inch (or a heaping ⅛" seam allowance) to accommodate the circle's curve.

Apply glue to the seam allowance, and use the magic wand to smooth the curves and eliminate the pokies. You'll need thirteen circles for the project.

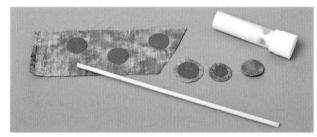

Trim and glue baste circles.

at last! the flowers

The flowers begin the same way as the leaves. Staple the flower template to the remaining folded freezer paper, placing staples inside each component piece. Following the lines on the photocopies, cut out the petals, and cut the petals away from the middle. Don't take out the staples yet.

As you cut out each piece, you may find it helpful to place it in its spot on the Key page. This will help you understand how the pieces fit together—this step is especially helpful with complex designs.

To get to the circle in the center, cut straight in from the edge of the F shape to the center. Carefully cut out the center along the line. Still leave those staples in for now.

Cut in toward center circle.

MANAGING MASS PRODUCTION

You may have noticed that the petals look alarmingly similar. You may also have noticed that the flower shapes are labeled with letters. I have a nifty little system that will help us keep track of where each freezer paper shape belongs, whether we're making one flower or hundreds.

Only pieces that must fit back together need labels. The leaves and berries don't need labels, because they are complete in themselves. Use letters to identify the shapes and use numbers to identify the layer of paper.

Rustle up petal A and a writing device. The staple remover will come in handy now, too. Carefully take out the staples without allowing the stack to spring apart. Peel off the photocopy layer, and set it aside.

The first layer of freezer paper is paper side up. Label it A1.

The second layer of freezer paper is plastic side up. Flip it over, and label it A2. Set it next to A1.

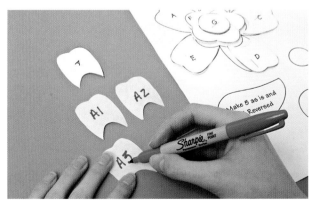

Label each shape.

The third layer is paper side up. Label it A3, and set it next to A2.

The fourth layer is plastic side up. Flip it over, and mark it A4.

The next layer is paper side up again. Label it A5, and set it next to A4.

And finally, we have plastic side up again. Flip it over, and mark it A6. And it goes, that's right, next to A5.

Toss the photocopy layer. It's done its job; let it enjoy retirement.

NOW TO THE B'S!

Let's tackle the B petal next. Remove the staples, and set aside the photocopy layer.

The first layer is paper side up. Label it B1, and put it on top of A1.

The next layer is plastic side up. Flip it over, and label it B2. It goes on top of A2.

Now we're back to paper side up. Label it B3, and put it with A3.

B's on top of A's

Getting the pattern here? Remember, the layers will be paper, plastic, paper, plastic. We've now made mirror-image flower templates, just as we did for the leaves. The subtle differences add interest to your quilts, especially those with more complex motifs.

Go ahead and label and sort the rest of the petals, the curvy middle, and the center circle. I'll wait.

To keep your freezer paper templates organized until you're ready for the next step, neaten up each stack and tack it together with a staple.

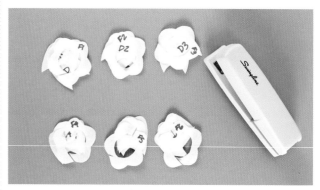

Staple tack the stacks.

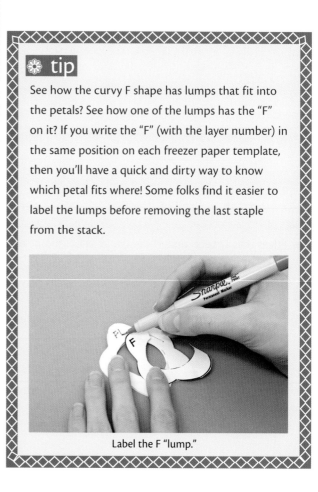

🌸 **tip**

See how the curvy F shape has lumps that fit into the petals? See how one of the lumps has the "F" on it? If you write the "F" (with the layer number) in the same position on each freezer paper template, then you'll have a quick and dirty way to know which petal fits where! Some folks find it easier to label the lumps before removing the last staple from the stack.

Label the F "lump."

PRESS TO THE FABRIC

Remove the staple from one stack of templates. Using a hot iron, press the shiny side of the freezer paper shapes to the wrong side of the fabrics you have chosen for the appliqué. Cut out around the freezer paper shapes, *adding* approximate ¼″ seam allowances as you cut. On the curvy F shape, wait to cut out the hole in the fabric for the center circle until after the outside edges are glue basted; this way the piece will be more stable and easier to cut and glue baste.

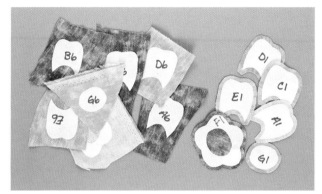

Cut, trim, and glue baste shapes, but don't cut center from F yet.

OVERS AND UNDERS

You're going to glue and then stitch the flowers together before you put them on the background. To do this, you have to decide which edges to glue baste and which to leave unbasted. This is the trickiest part, and you'll have to make this decision for each new design. But the more you appliqué, the easier it will become.

I think of these edges as "overs" and "unders." Edges that appear to be "over," or in front of another part of the design are called over edges. These edges get *glue basted over*. Edges that appear "under," or behind, another part of the design are called under edges and are left *unbasted*.

To make it easier, the Flower Key diagram (above right) has red lines that show which edges are under edges. Remember that some of our flowers are mirror imaged—when you place them on the Key, half will fit with the paper side up, the other half with the fabric side up.

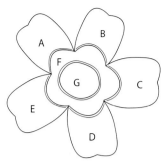

Flower Key indicating "under" edges in red.

For the flowers, glue baste the outside edges of the petals (which are *over* the background) but not the edge that touches the curvy F piece (because the petals seem to disappear *under* it).

Glue baste the edge of F that touches the petals, but not the edge that touches the center circle, which appears to be over the curvy F. And of course, glue baste the center circle.

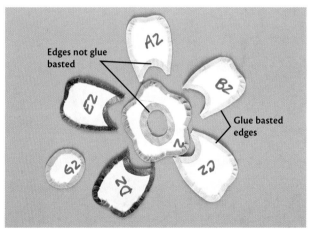

Edges not glue basted

Glue basted edges

Arrange glue-basted parts of flower.

DOCKING

Once you have your overs basted, it's time to glue the flower together. You want to glue the basted edges to the unbasted seam allowances without overlapping the freezer paper. I call this "docking" the shapes. When a boat is brought in to the dock, it should just kiss the pier. If it's too far away from the dock, the passengers have to jump (or swim!) to shore. Overdocking results in a repair bill for the boat and the pier!

Our goal is for the freezer paper edges to just kiss. I use a lightbox for this step, but any light source will work.

Working with the paper side up, apply glue to the basted seam allowance on the center circle G. Gently place the curvy F shape on top. The light shines through the seam allowance, making it easy to see how the pieces fit together.

Now smear glue on the basted edge of the curvy F shape. If you have put the F marking in the correct lump, the A petal will fit right on top of it. Again, let the light show you exactly where to place the petal. Depending on whether you're working with a right or left flower (remember creating those mirror images when we made the templates?), the lettered petals will follow clockwise (or counterclockwise) around that curvy F shape.

Take a closer look at the docking photo below. Notice how you can see a shadow through the paper on the "E" petal; that's an example of overdocking. The "B" petal shows a glow of light next to the paper; it's been underdocked. The "A" petal is just perfect.

Docking on lightbox

Glue baste and dock all the flowers for the project.

finally, we need some stems

There are at least 2,000 different ways to make appliqué stems. What follows is my favorite.

ON THE BIAS

To make stems that curve, cut your fabric strips on the bias. It doesn't have to be a perfect bias—close is good enough.

Find the 45° line on your rotary ruler. Align that with any straight edge on the stem fabric so that the cutting edge extends off the fabric on both ends. Cut the angle.

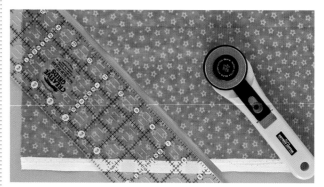

Cut stems on bias.

Now slide the ruler to the right until the 1″ measurement line is aligned with that freshly cut angle. Cut again to make a 1″-wide bias strip. For the *Ring O' Posies* project, you'll need several strips, ranging from a few inches to about 13″ long.

PRESS IN THIRDS

With a hot iron, press the bias strips into thirds, wrong sides together. Think of how you would fold a piece of paper to put into an envelope—that's how to fold the strip. To help the strip hold its shape, use spray sizing to spray the bias strip *before* pressing. Keep the iron only on the edge being pressed over.

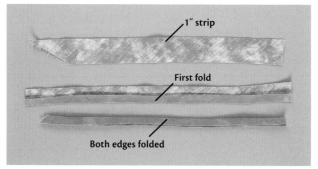

1″ strip

First fold

Both edges folded

Stems pressed in three stages

choosing a background

It's finally time to decide on the background for your appliqué. You can make a statement with a dramatically pieced background or with just one spectacular piece of fabric. You can let the appliqué rule the project by choosing a single, quiet background fabric to support your motifs. My favorite backgrounds are usually simply pieced (squares or rectangles) out of subtly different fabrics, playing peek-a-boo with the viewer. This is a sneaky way to add interest without detracting from the appliqué design.

> **note**
> The directions for piecing the background for *Ring O' Posies* are on page 39.

and now we stitch

Thread your sewing machine with invisible thread in the top and cotton thread in a neutral color in the bobbin. (I like 50-weight cotton, as it's less likely to be pulled to the front of the work.) You'll want a new 70/10 sharps needle and either a clear or open-toe foot on the machine.

The stitch you choose is very important. A traditional blind hem stitch adjusted to be very short and small is a good choice. **Important:** Start with *both the width and the length* set to 1.

Now, many machines won't let you adjust that stitch to be small enough. Some may allow you to make the stitch narrow enough, but they often have too many (more than three) stitches between the bites. Worry not, because the basic zigzag stitch is just as invisible. The initial settings for the zigzag are a *width of 1* and a *length of 2*.

I never use a blanket or buttonhole stitch. The straight-in-straight-out bite keeps the edge of the appliqué flat, making the stitch show more. For a perfectly invisible stitch, always use a V-shaped bite, whether it's a blind hem stitch or a zigzag. (Find more about threads and tweaking our machines in Chapter Four, pages 29–37).

Sew the flower motifs together before sewing them to the background. Anywhere an "over" edge overlaps an "under" edge gets stitched now.

Contrasting thread shows how stitches should land on appliqués.

ARRANGE AS DESIRED

Because all your appliqué pieces are sewn into finished motifs, you can place them on the background however you please, with no guessing about how they will actually fit. And there are no flapping seam allowances to mess up the spacing.

I like to move all the motifs around on the prepared background until they please me. For *Ring O' Posies*, I put the flowers in place first, tucked in the leaves next, and then placed the stems where they made sense.

Sample motif placement (pin with flat flower-head pins).

Pin every last bit of appliqué in place before you take a single stitch on the background. I really like flat flower-head pins for holding everything down. They are super sharp and extra long, and the flat heads don't fight with the freezer paper. Also, these pins hold the appliqués in place without distorting the shapes.

AT LAST, STITCH TO THE BACKGROUND

Begin stitching the appliqués to the background. Where you've tucked in leaves under flowers, you have two layers of freezer paper—don't stitch those areas just yet. For now, you're just stitching around the perimeter of the design.

Once that is done, work from the wrong side as you trim the background fabric from behind the appliqués, leaving a ¼" seam allowance. You only need to trim away the areas where the freezer paper (or office dots) lurk.

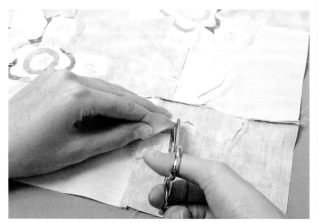

Trim away background fabric behind appliqués.

Now go back to the front of the work, and stitch the sections we skipped where the flowers overlap the leaves. This little extra step reduces the bulk in those seams (no background fabric is trapped) and makes it much easier to remove the freezer paper.

To remove the freezer paper templates, place the completed appliqué wrong side up on a firm surface. Cover it with a damp towel, and pat it down for good contact.

Let it sit for about 20 minutes to soften the glue. The freezer paper shapes should slide right out. If they don't, give them a few minutes more under the towel. The templates can be kind of slimy, so I work over a waste can and keep the damp towel nearby to wipe my hands.

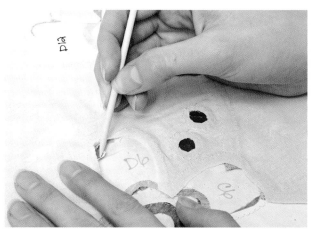

Use your "magic wand" (cuticle stick) to remove freezer paper.

Once you've removed all the freezer paper templates, immediately press the finished appliqué with a hot iron to dry it. Don't ever let it just air dry. Even prewashed fabric can run when left sitting wet.

Our basic appliqué is finished! How cool is that? Just wait until you see what we do next!.

All pressed and ready to go

Pieces of a Quilter's Life: Fabric Collecting

Back when I first moved to Saginaw, I traveled on a tour bus with the local guild to my very first national quilt show. I had actually been quilting for many years, but I had no idea that there were groups of people who got together to do quilt-y things. Until then, I had been home with four very active little boys, making quilts all by my lonesome.

After a three-hour ride, our bus dropped us at a door that led right into the vendor mall. I thought I had found quilting heaven! Never before had I seen so many retail therapy opportunities gathered in one place. For the next five hours, I made sure I visited as many booths as humanly possible. I saw gadgets of all sorts, rulers in every shape and size. And the fabric—oh, the fabric! Neat little fat quarter bundles, fabric collections of all styles and batiks, something I had never seen before. I left the building so laden with packages that I waddled like a two year old in her first snowsuit.

As I joined the line to board the bus, two quilters in front of me were discussing the beautiful quilts they had seen. Quilts? There were quilts? Who had time to look at quilts when there was so much shopping to do?!

In the many years since then, I've had the chance to take part in many organized shopping expeditions. Be they a formally arranged shop hop or an impromptu ride to the next town, I've learned that there is one question that may never be asked.

As our friends stand in line with bolts stacked to their chins we must never ask, "What are you going to do with that?" Fabric purchases require no justification! A stash must be carefully and constantly built. That's my story, and I'm sticking with it.

creative options

Y ou've just seen how quickly and easily you can prepare a bazillion freezer paper templates to create traditional quilts with repeating motifs. But what if you want to appliqué a subject with no repeats? With some very small changes, this technique still wins the day. I will use my *Still Life* project (page 42) to walk you through how easy it is to start with a simple line drawing.

(The specific fabric requirements and directions for the *Still Life* wallhanging are on page 43.)

create the templates

Let's take a moment to look at the *Still Life* project. Start by making photocopies of all four *Still Life* templates (pages 44–47). Make two full-size copies of the design—one to keep as a reference (your Key) and one to cut up to make the freezer paper shapes. To create the full-size pattern, cut on the dotted lines, and glue those edges to the adjacent sections, as shown in the diagram.

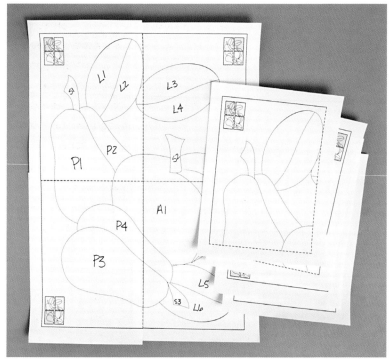

Glued-together pattern should look like this.

tip

If you're using a home scanner and inkjet printer, you can print one copy directly onto freezer paper. (Remember, do not use freezer paper in a copy machine or laser printer.) In this case, to have the finished design oriented just like the original line drawing, you'll need to reverse the design onto the freezer paper. Look for this option in the scanning or printing menus. Remember to also print a reference key on regular paper.

LABEL THE SHAPES

Even though the shapes are simple, we'll still mark and organize them before we begin cutting. It's so much easier to do it now than to have to guess where they belong later. The more complex the design, the more important this step is.

Instead of managing multiple repeats, for this project we just need to track placement, which requires a simpler labeling system. Each part gets its own number. So, let's use "P" for the pears, "A" for apple, "L" for leaf, and "S" for stem. (Brilliant, huh?) As I'm sure you've noticed, the labeling is already done for you on the template pages.

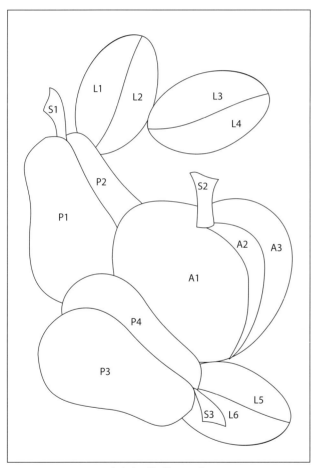

Labeled *Still Life* template

We'll consider the background separately a little later.

TEMPLATES FOR LARGE DESIGNS

For designs larger than our freezer paper, we can bond sections of the paper together to make a larger sheet. On a heat-safe surface, overlap the freezer paper pieces by about ½". Use the tip of the iron (or one of those mini craft irons) to fuse the paper together. For another, easier option, try Ricky Tims' Extra-Large Freezer Paper sheets, which are about 42 inches square (available from C&T Publishing; see Resources, page 80).

To have the finished design look just like the original line drawing, staple the photocopy to the shiny plastic side of the freezer paper. (Shiny side down will give you a mirror image.)

> ✿ **tip**
>
> Sometimes I'll cut two layers of freezer paper even though I only need one set of templates. I consider the second set an understudy in case I lose a piece or mangle it or change my mind on the fabric after it's already glued.

STAPLE AS YOU CUT

Remember to set aside one photocopy as the Key. Chunk away the background from the other. Don't cut on the lines just yet.

With a large design, you most likely will not be able to get a staple into all the parts before you start cutting. Never, ever roll the paper to staple an area! It distorts the paper and will result in nothing but grief. Instead, just staple what can be reached and then cut out those shapes, leaving a few stapled areas to hold everything together. Staple some more, then cut some more, until the job is done.

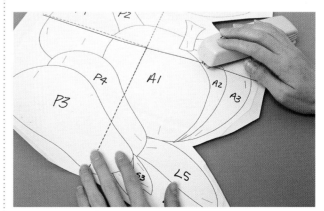

Keep stapling and cutting to reach all shapes.

As each shape is cut away from the design, place it, still stapled, on the corresponding shape on the Key. Not only will this help you stay organized, it will also help you see how the parts relate to the whole when you choose your fabrics.

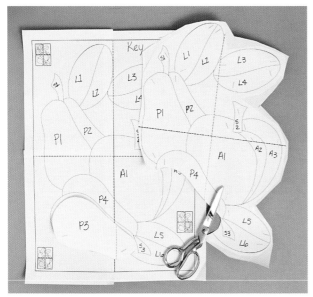

Cut shapes, and place on Key.

now to the fabric

Once the freezer paper templates are created, continue just as described in Chapter One (pages 4–14). Press the templates onto the wrong side of the fabric, then trim, glue baste, and dock them. Remember, for each internal edge, you need one over (glue-basted) edge and one under (unbasted) edge. It helps to think of the basted edge as the foreground edge: It's in front of the unbasted edge. Simply decide what's in front, and then glue baste that edge.

Sometimes an edge changes from an over to an under. Feel free to clip the seams to glue baste just the over part of a seam allowance.

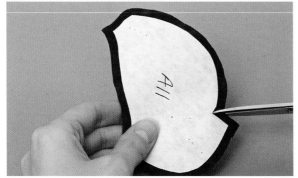

An over edge becomes an under edge, thanks to a simple clip.

WORK IN SECTIONS

Even though this project isn't made up of repeated motifs, we can still work in units. For *Still Life*, we can baste, dock, and stitch the apple together; baste, dock, and stitch each of the pears; and then do the same with the leaves. Finally, the completed motifs are basted, docked, and stitched together.

Completed sections docked and sewn.

Once the entire appliqué piece is stitched together, it's time to plunk it down on the background fabric. Because your design is essentially finished, it is very easy to move the stitched appliqué around on the fabric until you find the perfect spot for it. This part is especially fun on hand-dyed fabrics with lovely gradations of color and value.

When you're happy with the placement, all that's left to do is to stitch it to the background, remove the freezer paper, and quilt away.

Audition appliqué on background.

but wait! another approach

The project has been fun so far, but it's kind of simple—almost coloring-bookish. Would you believe that without drawing a single additional line you can easily create more interest and dimension?

ADD INTEREST TO A SIMPLE DESIGN

We can start with basic shapes and add interest by cutting the simple shapes into sexy segments.

Here is our *Still Life* again. But this time we'll make it a bit more detailed. This look is achieved by simply cutting our freezer paper templates into smaller bits.

Extra sections in this version of *Still Life* add dimension to shapes.

The leaves are easy, so let's start with "L1". Cut this template into three curvy segments. So that you don't have to worry about keeping track of them, label them "L1a", "L1b", and "L1c". Label the Key, too, so you have an idea of where these pieces belong. Similarly, cut shape "L2" into three segments.

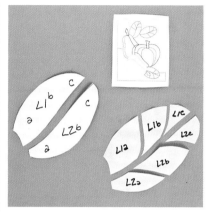

Cut leaf templates into segments.

The new apple has bright sections added to make it rounder, plus a nifty little dark area for the pear's shadow. Just for fun, the background was treated like an appliqué motif that was cut from freezer paper and appliquéd together, just like the fruit. Deciding how to cut it was as simple as giving the fruit a table on which to sit (using a darker fabric also added weight to the bottom of the piece), as well as a little shadow to one side.

The secret to cutting natural contours is very simple. You want to add lines that echo, but don't exactly repeat, the shape of the edges. Curves taper to disappear around a rounded edge. As highlights move to the front of a curved shape, the lines straighten a bit.

In nature, straight lines are very rare and are almost never seen in living things. Gentle curves win the day. Then again, many quilters fill shapes with jagged edges and corners and create a beautiful work of art. Your own design only needs to please *you* to be "done right."

Play around by cutting up the simple *Still Life* shapes; you're risking only a little paper and smidges of fabric. It's another way to experience appliqué—unplanned and spontaneous. And when you've finished with your fruit appliqués, have fun moving them from background to background until they find their perfect home. Then, stitch them down!

beyond freezer paper

The biggest drawback to using freezer paper is that it has to be removed. Oh, the gasps of horror that I hear in class when I tell students they will be cutting away the background fabric!

In all my many years of using this technique, I have never (no, never) had an appliqué fall off a quilt. Cutting away the background does not weaken the quilt in any way. The paper removal process is the quickest step and is pretty much mindless, so it doesn't bother me a bit.

But the quilt industry is a wonderful thing, constantly inventing spiffy new products for us to love.

WASH-AWAY APPLIQUÉ SHEETS

For some time we quilters have had water-soluble paper that we can use instead of freezer paper, and it works okay. Without a fusible side, this paper must first be glued to the fabric and then glue basted—a fiddly process. But now C&T has come out with Wash-Away Appliqué Sheets (see Resources, page 80). This iron-on stabilizer will soften and practically disappear with washing. In other words, it's like water-soluble freezer paper. I know! How awesome is that?

C&T Wash-Away Appliqué Sheets

Now I'm pretty frugal. For a lot of our appliqué projects, grocery store freezer paper will continue to work just fine. But this new stuff began life as a stabilizer. It allows us to do so much more than just skip the last step in this appliqué technique. Read on to see the amazing new options available.

trapuntoed appliqué

Padded, or trapuntoed, appliqué adds a beautiful, dimensional quality to a quilt.

Using appliqué sheets instead of the more traditional freezer paper lets you trap a layer of batting between the appliqué and the background, creating trapuntoed appliqué without taking a single extra stitch!

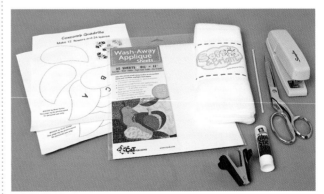

Tools and materials

BEGIN WITH THE TEMPLATES

I designed *Coxcomb Quadrille* (page 48) to take advantage of the stabilizer technique. The paper templates for this quilt (page 51) are prepared in exactly the same way as those for *Ring O' Posies* (pages 38–40). As with freezer paper, we can stack six layers of the appliqué sheets, shiny sides together (that's where the fusible part is), and staple the paper templates in place.

Take extra care when cutting this stuff. Appliqué sheets are softer than freezer paper, so it's easier to crush the edges together. Use your best, sharpest scissors to get the crispest edges.

Label and sort the motifs just as we did with the posies. I like to use a pencil to address these shapes, that way there is no worry about ink migrating when washed.

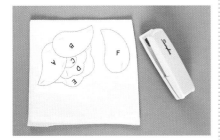

Label and staple templates.

Take care when positioning templates made from appliqué sheets on the fabric. Whereas freezer paper shapes can be peeled off and relocated, these stick for good once you've applied the hot iron.

Trim, glue baste, and dock the motifs. Stitch the docked parts together.

THE PADDING LAYER

It's a matter of personal preference how much loft you should tuck under the shapes. Too little, and it's hardly worth the effort. Too much, and the shapes will look uncomfortably bloated.

To determine the right batting for *Coxcomb Quadrille*, I made several extra motifs. Using every different type of batting I could get my hands on (and double layers of some), I stitched all the motifs to a background; then I quilted and bound the quilt. Then I washed the quilt repeatedly.

Batting test quilt

Soft & Bright from the Warm Company turned out to be my favorite batting. It had just enough loft to fill the spaces without making the piece looked over-stuffed. It was also extremely easy to cut. I could even cut two layers at one time, making it quick and easy to create enough batting pieces for my whole project.

CUTTING THE BATTING LAYER

To cut out the batting shapes, we'll need to create a template that is just a smidge smaller than the finished motif. Simply trace the perimeter of the appliqué shape, and then trim away about ⅛" all around.

Paper templates are too stiff and cumbersome to use with batting. Instead, cut the template from contrasting fabric. Use lots of spray sizing to stiffen the fabric before cutting the template. Use flat flower-head pins to hold the template in place so that you don't distort the shape while you cut out the batting.

A heavy smear of glue on the wrong side of the appliqué motifs will hold the batting in place. Position the motifs, and stitch them to the background, just as you did before. Discard the fabric templates. And you're done!

To emphasize the trapuntoed shapes, choose a dense quilting design for the background. Don't be afraid to quilt through the extra batting. This is a sneaky way to add even more dimension and excitement to your appliquéd designs.

Fabric template (left) cut slightly smaller than appliqué outline.
Pin fabric template to batting (right), and cut out shapes.

Pieces of a Quilter's Life: Dudley Do-It-Rights

We all know someone who is a perfectionist; some of us may even see one in the mirror every morning. And, oh my, aren't they just a little proud of it? Perfectionists can't help but feel smugly superior to us poor slobs who will settle for just any old thing.

In fact, not only must it be perfect, it must be achieved just so. These Dudley Do-It-Rights operate on the assumption that there is just one right way to do everything, and, of course, it's the way they do it.

People who already know the right way to do everything surely spoil the fun for the rest of us. Instead of being open to new ideas and techniques, they have slammed shut their minds and hearts. When a new process is presented, old Dudley replies with a haughty claim that it's cheating. Anything worth doing is worth doing right. Oh, please!

As a recovering perfectionist, I can tell you, it's really nothing to be proud of. Instead, perfectionists are really *im*perfectionists. All that perfectionists see are the flaws, the failures to live up to ridiculously high standards. They are never satisfied. It's a sad way to be. Imagine doing really great work on a project only to dwell on the one small area that disappointed. Perfectionists can rarely accept a compliment without answering, "Yes, but . . ."

My new goal is to simply do my best each day. Not *the* best, but *my* best, and that best changes each day. Letting go of perfection means I'm free to make mistakes. I can try new things and be patient with myself as I build my skills. My new motto is: Anything worth doing is worth doing badly for as long as it takes. And the very worst thing that can happen is that I may have to buy more fabric. It's a risk I'm willing to take.

fabric & color

When it comes to choosing fabric, quilters seem to fall into two camps: those who love it, and those who dread it. What separates the two, in my opinion, is merely confidence, or the lack of it.

Color theory for us quilters can be as complicated as we want to make it. Sure, a little knowledge of the color wheel can get us out of a jam. If a design is a little boring, I add something from the opposite side of the wheel. For example, my red and green quilts, like *Coxcomb Quadrille* (page 48), almost always improve with a punch of yellow. Or, if all of my fabrics are cool colors, I'll toss in a little heat, or vice versa.

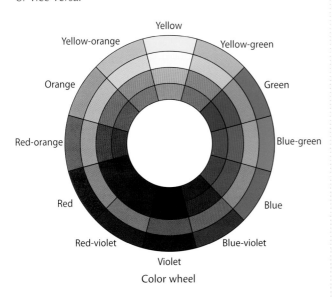

Color wheel

talk about value

What's more important to me than color is value. I've said it before, and I'll say it again:

Value does all the work, and color gets all the credit.

Value is what we often think of as the shade, the saturation, or the depth of the color. For purists, "shade" means something else. But we're not purists; we're just appliquérs trying to make our quilts more interesting.

Using value in appliqué is a wonderful way to give a project depth and realism. Of course, not every appliqué project needs that. In fact, many traditional quilts have nothing to do with realism, and that's just fine by me. But, even if realistic appliqué isn't our goal, a mix of values will make our quilts sparkle.

A QUILT THAT IS ALL MEDIUMS IS NEITHER RARE NOR WELL DONE

Most of the fabrics available in quilt shops are medium in value. An awful lot of fabric collections, though they feature lovely colors and interesting prints, are just a mishmash of one value.

A quilt that engages us and piques our interest is one that will keep the eye moving. A quilt that is all medium-value fabrics allows us to understand the quilt in a quick glance, and off we go. Close or minimal contrast between fabrics makes for a soothing, quiet, homey quilt, terrific for cuddle quilts because it doesn't challenge us. But toss in a light or dark fabric, or better yet both, and the quilt comes alive. High-contrast quilts can be lively, even jarring, but they are usually the quilts that get and keep our attention.

OUR MAGICAL EYES

The thing about value is that it is relative. A fabric can be dark with one set of companions and light with another. It can be a challenge sometimes to get the values of a range of fabrics sorted out. Notice how the curved arrow in the following illustration appears to change value depending on the surroundings. I use a couple of tricks when my project needs special attention to value.

The medium value arrow can be both light and dark, depending on its company.

We have all the tools we need to discern value right in our heads. Our eyes have these magical things called rods and cones, which act together to give us vision. The cones perceive color. Without them, we'd be dogs. (Well, that and the opposable thumbs, and the fur.) The rods differentiate value and, on their own, would limit our vision to black and white.

The cool thing is that the cones need a certain level of light in order to do their job. Have you ever noticed that colors disappear at twilight? We can put that to work for us.

✿ tip

Back in the day, when I was working at a local quilt shop, my students would ask for my help in picking fabrics. The shop owners thought something shady was going on when customers would approach me at the counter and ask if I'd go in the bathroom with them. A perfectly innocent request when they understood that it was the only place dark enough to let our rods do the work! We would giggle for a few minutes while our eyes adjusted and then giggled some more as we rearranged the fabrics in value order.

CREATE VALUE STUDIES

For quilt designs that rely heavily on value to achieve the desired outcome, like the yellows in the blooms in *Saginaw Sunflowers* (page 65), I create a value study. Doesn't that sound all artsy? (It's all in how you name it, huh?) It just means that I spend a little more time assigning value to the fabrics I wish to use.

I begin by pulling a bunch of fabrics from my stash. I sort them out and line them up in my best guess from light to dark on my ironing board or cutting table. Then I wait for dark. I have uncovered windows on all four sides of the studio, so simply putting out the lights is not an option. I kind of like the idea of waiting: it slows down the heat of the project and gives me more time to think about the work—something to anticipate.

Fabrics, waiting for (almost) dark

But sometimes deadlines reign supreme, and waiting isn't an option. A very quick way to determine value is to lay out the fabric on the bed of a scanner or photocopy machine and make a black-and-white copy. Taking the color out of the equation makes it super simple to see which fabric is really darker.

Scan fabrics, refine the order, and scan again.

Sometimes I just spread out the yardage, straight from the stash. Other times I'll cut a small rectangle from each fabric, maybe 1″ × 3″ or so, and attach it to cardstock with double-stick tape. Either way, I can easily rearrange the order of the fabrics as the printouts dictate.

Another easy tool for determining value is a digital camera. Most can be set to take black-and-white pictures. Using the digital preview in black and white is another quick way to sort out fabrics by value.

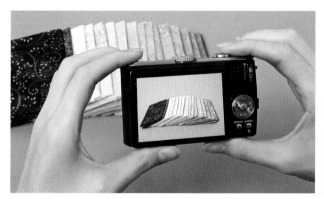

Fabric viewed through digital camera

Lots of folks like to use the colored plastic value finders. If they work for you, I'm all for it. But to be honest, I've never had much success with them. Basically, they require advance planning so that I have them with me when I'm shopping, and I'm all for accidental fabric procurement opportunities.

THE RULE OF FIVE

Once the fabrics are in value order, I divide them into five values: light, light medium, medium, dark medium, and dark. For most projects, I may choose only one fabric to represent each category. In other projects, however, I may use several fabrics in each value category, especially when a scrappy look is the goal. When I'm dealing with just a few fabrics, or if I've cut the smaller fabric rectangles, I'll just mark up the cardstock. If I'm using a bazillion

fabrics, an address label or office sticky dot on the fabric helps me keep track of their assigned values. (Saves on a lot of wondering what I was thinking later.) My system is really simple: Light = L, Light Medium = M−, Medium = M, Dark Medium = M+, Dark = D.

Labeled fabric

For *Saginaw Sunflowers* (page 65), I chose one set of five for the full-face flowers and a different set of five for the profile flowers. This is a great way to use little bits of lots of fabrics without ending up with a jangled mess.

> ### 🌸 tip
>
> Don't forget to consider both sides of the fabric! Sometimes that perfect shade can be found on what is commonly called the "wrong side." I think that's rather shortsighted. Using both sides of the fabric doubles our fabric stashes instantly! The bottom center sections of the *Saginaw Sunflowers* pail use the "wrong" side of the fabric. I don't think it looks wrong at all.

SUNSHINE AND SHADOW

One of my favorite ways to play with value in a project is to imply a light source, like sunlight streaming through a window. My designs are often simple, but playing with value in the motifs can give those designs more dimension and interest.

Suggesting sunshine is as easy as considering which petals of the flower would be in bright light, which would fall into deep shade, and what to do with the ones that are neither.

In *Saginaw Sunflowers*, because I really wanted to show sunshine on the bouquet, I took the time to make a plan for fabric placement. First I decided what I wanted to be light, medium, and dark. As I cut out the freezer paper shapes, I added the labels "L", "M−", "M", "M"+, or "D" on each template to help me remember what I decided.

Saginaw Sunflowers labeled template

Even though I needed only three of each style of flower, I made six template sets, reasoning that I could substitute one of the extra petals if my fabric choices needed tweaking. (If you've created mirror image motifs for an appliqué, odd-numbered petals can replace other odd-numbered petals, and evens can replace evens.)

While usually I dive in and sew together the motifs right away, in this case I waited until all the sunflowers were docked together. Then I tried them out on the background to be sure I was really happy with the value placements in each part of the design. Then I sewed the motifs together.

The bottom line is that color matters less when value is used to advantage. When designing quilts, I rarely work in color. Instead, by using shades of gray as placeholders, I can create a design that will work with almost any color palette.

Grayscale design for *Rose Garland* (page 71)

Grayscale design for *Rose Garland* (page 71)

> ### ❋ tip
>
> If I had my choice, I would never publish a quilt pattern in color. Those flashy color pattern covers require quilters to translate my fabric choices to theirs. Often we see a design that gets our hearts aflutter, but we hate the fabrics shown. Simply take the pattern cover to the copy machine and make a black-and-white copy. Now it's easy to see how the values work in the design, and it will be much easier to create your own special version.

fabric styles

Many of us have styles of fabric that are our favorites. And then other styles just make us want to hurl. I love almost all sorts of fabric (and have the stash to prove it). Be it period fabric (Civil War, 1930s feed-sack, or mid-century modern), color type (pastels, brights, or "dirty" brown), or batiks (be still my heart!), they all live happily in my stash. I've never met a tone on tone that I couldn't love.

WE LOVE OUR STASHES

A stash is to a quilter what a vocabulary is to a writer.

It would be hard to imagine that anyone but Dr. Seuss could manage an interesting book with fewer than fifty different words. While *Green Eggs and Ham* is a great read if you're eight, devoted readers long to delve into meatier tomes.

So it is with our fabric stashes. Necessity may require that some quilters limit the volume of their stashes. Indeed, I keep my stash on the small size, but I do so by buying smaller, rather than fewer, cuts. In fact, the majority of the time, I purchase fat quarters. For fabrics that lend themselves to being used as background, I might buy a yard or two. And for really sensational fabrics (for me that would be anything with metallic prints), I go all out and buy as many yards as my budget allows.

My fat quarter shelf (Photo by Kent Ferrier)

Buying the smaller cuts solves so many problems. They don't take up as much space, allowing me a larger assortment. I'm also not as hesitant to cut into them. (What is it about a five-yard piece that draws a sweat when we consider using a quarter yard of it?) I don't have to love the fat quarter, either. If it's just a fat quarter, liking it is enough to bring it home with me. It's not as big a commitment, allowing me to take chances with fabric that may have a little more character than I might otherwise choose.

When it comes to fabric, the solution to pollution is dilution. If one fabric, color, or value grabs too much attention, adding more is almost always the answer.

LET THE FABRIC SET THE TONE

Notice how in the *Rose Garland* wallhanging the tone is set by the fabric choices. The Civil War–era fabrics are pretty much all medium value, making this a cozy, country style.

Civil War version of *Rose Garland*

In the bright fabric version of the same quilt, the pastels and soft brights, also mostly medium values, lend a cheery, whimsical look.

Brights version of *Rose Garland*

PLAYING WITH SILK

Okay, I'll admit it, I'm a sucker for silk. There's a depth to it. The colors are rich and full. Dupioni silk, with its glorious slubs, has incredible texture. While silk fabrics may seem exotic when compared to our common cottons, there are only a couple of small differences to consider.

Most quilt shop fabrics have been treated with special finishes to preserve the color and reduce the chance of dye running. Silks have not had this same treatment, however. For a quilt that is to be laundered, it is worthwhile to toss a bit of the silk into the washer to see if the colors run. In my experience, this has not been a big problem, but I'd surely rather know before I spent the time making a queen-sized quilt.

Dupioni silks lose a bit of their texture when washed. Because I value the texture as much as the color, I like to use these fabrics in wall quilts that won't be laundered. Instead of freezer paper, which needs to be wet to remove, I use C&T Wash-Away Appliqué Sheets for my templates.

So now you've created an appliquéd quilt top using the colors and fabrics that you love. While this is an excellent time to step back and admire our appliqué, we still have one more consideration. In Chapter Four we'll discover how we can add even more pizzazz to our appliqué. Let's play with thread!

Silk version of *Rose Garland*

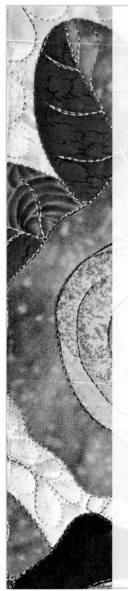

Pieces of a Quilter's Life: The Six-Trip Quilt

The house where I live was built before 1860. We like to think of it as more of a hobby than a home. There is always something that needs repair, replacement, or renovation. My hubby is one of those terrific handyman types, capable of just about any kind of construction work—the perfect guy to live with in an old house.

After many years of marriage, I've learned that presenting the next project in the right way improves the chances of getting it done. Instead of just saying that I want something done, I start out by asking how hard it would be to put a shower in the downstairs bathtub or add a garbage disposal to the kitchen sink or turn the attached garage into a studio. It gets him thinking positively from the start.

Kent has an interesting way of rating the difficulty of a job. After some consideration, he'll proclaim that this next project is probably a four-trip job. It will take four trips to the hardware store to gather the materials required to complete the project. He reasons that it's impossible to know everything he'll need until he gets into the job.

I think he's brilliant. I've begun to consider my quilt projects in a whole new way. I can tell already that my next quilt is easily a six-trip quilt! Who says we have to have every single piece of fabric picked out before we can start? I think it's perfectly reasonable to keep adding fabrics until the last stitch in the binding is taken. And even then, we may want something special for the label.

So what if we gather enough fabric to make the project three times over? How could leftover fabric ever be a bad thing? Surely a day will come when we will be grateful to have that sky fabric tucked into our stash. It will provide the perfect starting place for our next project, if only we can remember to take it on that first trip.

thread

Oh, how we quilters love to hate invisible thread—and probably with good reason. Poor-quality monofilament thread can be a nightmare to sew with. If the thread is old, it can become twirly and cranky and wrap its sorry self all over the machine's thread guides, messing up the tension—both the machine's and ours!

Today's monofilament threads are far superior to the fishing line we used so many years ago. One of the best innovations has been the creation of polyester invisible thread. Polymonofilament thread doesn't stretch as much, yellow, or melt the way nylon thread can. It's also a lot more forgiving in the sewing machine.

Let's start with an in-depth look at helping our machines play nicely with invisible thread. After that, we'll look at the fun and games we can enjoy with other types of threads.

playing with stitches

Just as people who hand appliqué pride themselves on their perfect, invisible stitches, we machine artists need to take the time to perfect the settings on our sewing machines. A few simple strategies will ensure that our appliqué is just as lovely as our hand-stitching counterpart's.

THREAD THE MACHINE

Now would be a great time to pull out the machine manual and review our machine's threading path. It's so easy to become sloppy as we become more familiar with our machines. And yet beautifully invisible stitches require proper threading.

In my experience, invisible thread seems to be happier on an upright spindle. The horizontal spindles sometimes put an unwanted twist into the thread. That said, sometimes the upright spool lets the thread spill off and wind around the spindle. This spool recoil is caused by the stop-and-start sewing that comes with carefully stitching around appliqué shapes. The pooling of thread can cause serious tension issues, and even broken needles! A felt pad or sponge at the base of the spindle helps. (So that's what those things were for.)

The best solution to most thread problems is a thread stand, also known as a cone holder. The thread floats up to the thread mast and over to the machine, happily making its way to the needle. A thread stand helps with all sorts of specialty threads. Be sure to buy one that has a heavy base. They are harder to knock over.

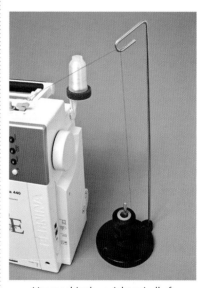

Use machine's upright spindle for invisible thread, or use a thread stand, which solves most thread problems.

For the bobbin, my preference is to use 50-weight cotton. It's much fatter than the invisible thread, making it more likely to stay on the back of the work instead of pulling up through the needle hole. Choose a neutral color—say, a soft off-white or a medium gray.

I'm not a big fan of using invisible thread, especially nylon, in the bobbin. If wound too tightly, the thread can actually stretch and warp the bobbin, which can damage the hook and race of the machine.

ADJUST THE STITCH

When many people think of the basics of machine appliqué, their initial reaction is often that the blind hem stitch is the *right* stitch to use. Anything else is second rate. I'm here to tell you that's just not true.

Many machines just won't allow us to make this stitch small enough to do a good job. On some machines, there are so many straight stitches between the bites that it's next to impossible to get the bites close enough together.

The blind hem stitch

To determine if the blind hem stitch on your machine is the right choice, look for a stitch with three or fewer straight stitches between the bites. Because it's preferable that the bites come from right to left, it is useful to be able to mirror image the stitch. Being able to move the needle position to the far right also helps, because it's easier to get the stitching line in the correct position when you can use the inside edge of the foot as a guide.

You'll need to reduce the size of the stitch. The initial settings are:

Width of 1, Length of 1

Every machine is different, so you can expect to do some tweaking. The straight stitch part should fall on the *under* edges, with the left side of the needle brushing the folded edge of your appliqués. The bites should just grab a few threads of that edge of the appliqué and should be no more than ⅛" apart.

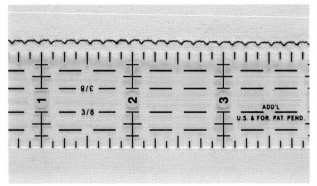

Blind hem stitch sample

The lowly zigzag

The reaction to the zigzag stitch is always the same, as if a quilter had to settle for a second-rate stitch because the *right* one doesn't work. This is especially true of quilters who have spent lots of dollars on their machines. Oh, the weeping and gnashing of teeth!

Let me promise you—the zigzag stitch is an excellent choice. It's every bit as invisible as the blind hem stitch. It's even a little more forgiving. And, as you'll see later in this chapter, it can be used with other types of thread for special effects.

So, with a zigzag stitch, the starting settings are:

Width of 1, Length of 2

We're looking for a stitch that looks more like a drunken straight stitch than a satin stitch. The majority of this stitch falls on the appliqué. When the needle is in the *under* edge fabric, the left side of the needle should brush over the *over* edge fold. The bites should swing just a few threads onto the over edge. Like the blind hem stitch, we want the bites to be no more than ⅛" apart. Moving the needle to the right, if possible, will also help get the stitch placed just so.

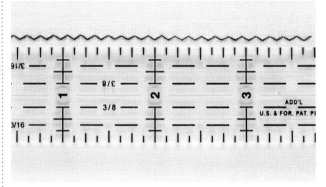

Zigzag stitch sample

Other stitches

I've learned from experience that the bite needs to be V-shaped. It's that V shape in the stitch that helps the stitch disappear. When the freezer paper is removed (or the stabilizer is washed away), the edges of the appliqué plump up, and the V-shaped bite allows that to happen. Bites that come straight in and back out again pile up the thread and flatten the appliqué edge, making the stitch show more. Even if your machine manual calls a stitch like that an appliqué stitch, it's not the best choice.

ADJUST THE TOP TENSION

Before we dive into stitching together our motifs, it makes sense to test drive the stitches. Test the stitch on three layers of fabric—a single layer will look horrible no matter what. We don't need to stitch over an edge—any scrap of fabric will do. Just stitch out a couple of inches and then check the quality. (It's easiest to examine from the bobbin side.) If the stitch is the right size, then flip back to the front and look for evidence of bobbin thread on the top.

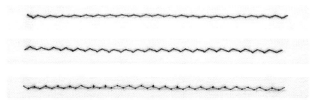

Samples of tension issues: top tension too loose (top);
tension just right (middle); top tension too tight (bottom)

The stitch should lie happily on the fabric. If it feels raised or rough, like a scar, that's a sure sign that the tension needs to be adjusted.

If bobbin thread shows on the top side, your first adjustment will be to the top tension, because the needle thread is pulling the bobbin thread to the top. If you lower/loosen the top tension, the bobbin thread should disappear. To loosen, move the tension dial to a lower number, adjusting it about a half increment at a time. Some machines require a very low setting—that's okay.

ADJUST THE BOBBIN TENSION

Sometimes you just can't get there by adjusting only the top tension. But changing the bobbin tension doesn't have to be scary. For machines with a bobbin case, it's easy to give that adjustment screw a little turn. Drop-in bobbins have a case too—it's where the bobbin is popped into the machine. Remove the throat plate, and you'll find that you can remove the bobbin case for adjusting. Talk to your machine dealer to learn how to make the adjustments on your machine.

Drop-in bobbin case and regular bobbin case

The old saw of "righty-tighty, lefty-loosey" will help you remember which way to turn the adjustment screw. I think of the slot in the screw head as the hands on a clock, and I adjust five minutes at a time. Five minutes ago will loosen the tension; five minutes from now will tighten the tension. If the bobbin thread shows on top, you want to fast-forward to the future, just a smidge at a time.

For the faint of heart: Purchase an additional bobbin case to mess with and mark it with a dot of fingernail polish (anything else will wear off). Some machine brands have developed specialty bobbins for working with thicker threads. But we're getting ahead of ourselves; we'll consider bobbin work shortly.

IT'S ALL ABOUT THE NEEDLE

When a stitch is ugly, the first suspect is the needle. Even with a good-quality brand of needles, it's possible to have one that is bad right out of the package. One of my students once spent 30 minutes trying to thread a needle that was punched side to side instead of front to back.

Fine 70/10 needles allow us to snuggle right up to the edge of the appliqué. With these needles, the stitch can be smaller and easier to hide. A 60/8 needle isn't necessarily better. This size is often too fine and can snap on those areas with seam allowance buildup, like the points on leaves.

Needle should snuggle up to appliqué edge.

Sharps needles were designed for sewing on woven fabrics. The sharp point on the needle allows it to pierce easily through all the fabric, paper, and glue layers we've piled up.

READY, SET, SEW

Once we've made our machines happy, we can start by stitching our motifs together. I try to find a path that will allow me to catch the most pieces in the appliqué. I don't worry about backstitching to secure the stitches when using the blind hem stitch. Those little straight stitches between the bites are so tiny; I dare you to pull them out!

For the zigzag, I hold the work in place just long enough to make a tiny bar tack, no more than two passes, and then I allow the feed dogs to advance the work.

beyond invisible thread

The biggest selling point with invisible thread is that it matches everything. Two spools, one clear and one smoke-colored, will pretty much stitch out everything. For years, our alternative thread selection was very limited, making monofilament thread (despite its challenges) the best choice for invisible machine appliqué.

Today, lots of new thread companies are developing dozens of new threads. Our choices have really exploded. So let's play! Let's start with threads that will disappear, giving our appliqués that delicious hand-stitched look.

WE LOVE OUR ZIGZAG!

With anything other than invisible thread, the straight stitches of a blind hem stitch will show along the edge of the appliqué, making the stitch more obvious. For the most invisible stitches, let's use the zigzag stitch. (See, I told you it was a great stitch!)

For stitches that will disappear, you'll want to choose a thread that is very fine. It will also need to come as close as possible to matching the color of the *over* edge fabric.

Some of my current favorite threads include:

- Bottom Line polyester by Superior
- Deco Bob polyester by WonderFil Threads
- Silk thread by YLI and/or Clover
- 100-weight cotton by Aurifil
- 60/2 fine embroidery by Mettler

Selection of thread

Each brand includes dozens of colors in many shades. The silk threads are the most limited collections. Hand appliquérs enjoy collecting dozens of spools of threads for their projects, and I see no reason why they should have all the fun.

My *Carnations, Anyone?* sample was stitched using several shades of pink and green Bottom Line thread and a zigzag. If you look really closely, you'll see that the thread does show in some areas but completely disappears in most.

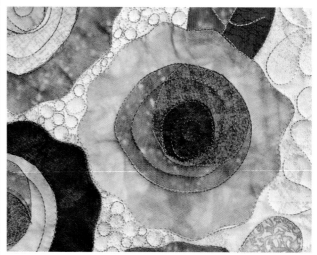
In *Carnations, Anyone?*, the pink Bottom Line thread plays peek-a-boo on the different shades of pink.

now we see it

Just because our original goal was a stitch that hides away, it doesn't mean that a stitch that shows is against the rules. Far from it! In fact, turned edges and docked shapes are the perfect stage for showy threads and stitches. With no raw edges to detract from the finish, we can celebrate beautiful threads and fancy stitches.

I'm blessed to have a nice sewing machine. It does all sorts of cool things, many I have never tried. Most of the time, it's set on a plain old straight stitch, perfect for piecing and quilting, but C&T Wash-Away Appliqué Sheets allow me to play with the machine's decorative stitches in a way that I never could with freezer paper.

THE *CALICO CAT*

There are three versions of my *Calico Cat* (pages 56–57). The *Groovy Kitty* was appliquéd using WonderFil's Deco Bob polyester threads in black with a zigzag stitch. The thread disappears very well on the black background but gives a lovely, wiggly edge on the other fabrics. The stitches are small and subtle and don't really contribute to the project's final look.

Stitching on *Groovy Kitty*
(full quilt on page 57)

Our *Country Kitten* was appliquéd using Presencia's rayon threads, using a blanket stitch and other decorative stitches along the turned edges. The stitches play a more important part in this design, adding a homey touch to the traditional fabrics.

Decorative stitching on *Country Kitten* (full quilt on page 57)

And then there is our *Victorian Cat*. My, isn't she fancy? The fabric is from Cherrywood, whose hand-dyeing process results in not-quite-solid colors with a yummy suede look, a perfect backdrop for decorative threads of all types. Decorative stitches were used not only on the edge of the appliqués but also within the shapes to create embroidered fabric.

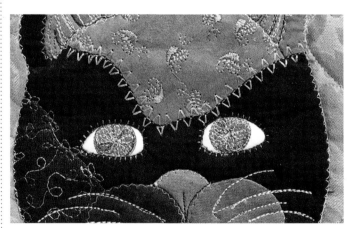

Decorative stitching on *Victorian Cat* (full quilt on page 56)

To support these decorative stitches, we'll use a double layer of the appliqué sheets. The layers can be tacked together first with a cool iron before the shapes are cut out. Or we can just cut two layers of the appliqué sheets at once (as if we were planning to make two cats just alike) and press them both to the wrong side of the fabric at the same time.

Trim the fabric, leaving a seam allowance. Pinch the edges (as when glue basting, but without the glue) as a guide for stitching. We want to keep the stitches only in the areas supported by the appliqué sheets. Once the decorative stitching is done, we can glue baste, dock, and stitch together our fancy cat.

SPECIALTY THREADS

The real secret to successfully using specialty threads lies in choosing the right needle for the job. My favorites are top-stitching and jeans needles. Needles designed especially for metallic threads will make stitching out those finicky threads a lot easier too.

When it comes to specialty threads such as metallic, Mylar, or rayon, buy the very best quality threads you can afford. Poorly made threads may seem like a bargain until they have us pulling out our hair in frustration. We can trust our local quilt shop or sewing machine shop to guide us to threads that will enhance our project without a fight.

CHOOSING THE BEST STITCHES

Before we can decide what thread to use, we need to choose our stitches. A design made up of tiny stitches will look choppy if stitched with threads that are too thick, so use thinner threads for this type of decorative stitch. Thicker threads, however, are terrific for satin stitch designs, which we'll see later in this chapter, or for designs made up of long stitches.

Before diving into the project pieces, practice stitching out the patterns on a scrap of fabric backed with two layers of stabilizer. That way, you can decide if you have the right stitch and thread combination, and you can make sure that the tension is adjusted properly for the prettiest stitches.

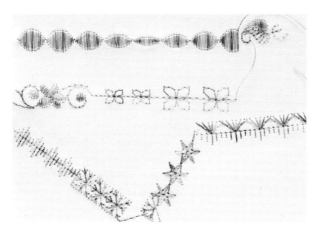

Practice scrap with decorative stitches

As mentioned earlier, to keep the bobbin thread from showing on top, your choices are to loosen the top tension or tighten the bobbin tension—and sometimes both.

I still like to use my standard 50-weight cotton in the bobbin. The fat thread stays on the back and shows less in the needle holes, and the toothy cotton nabs the decorative thread and holds it in place. That said, if the specialty thread is acting up, try changing to a polyester thread designed as bobbin fill. Sometimes it's a matter of finding a combination of threads that will play together nicely.

BOBBIN WORK FOR DETAILS AND DRAMA

Hand appliquérs love to use embroidery to embellish their appliqué. Bobbin work can give machine users the same result. We tend to think that bobbin work is mysterious and difficult, but nothing could be further from the truth. We've already discovered how easy it is to adjust the bobbin tension. Now all we have to do is remember to stitch with the wrong side up. Okay, so there may be a little more to it than that, but not much, really!

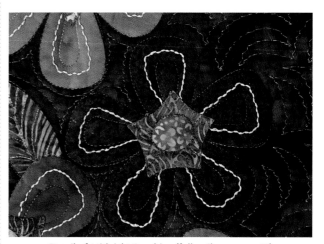

Detail of *Midnight Sunshine* (full quilt on page 60)

Choosing the best threads

I have to admit that I've wound all sorts of stuff onto a bobbin, even worsted weight yarn (which I don't recommend). Perle cotton, as thick as size 5, is a perfect candidate for bobbin work. I've even used twelve-strand silk embroidery floss with great success.

Your machine manual will probably insist that these types of threads should be hand-wound onto the bobbin. If the thread is stretchy, as yarn would be, hand winding is a good plan. If the thread isn't stretchy, however, I'd probably try winding the bobbin on the machine. A really thick yarn will fill a bobbin very quickly, so fiddling with trying to wind it on the machine would be kind of silly.

Two rules for bobbin work success

Rule 1: The thicker the thread, the looser the bobbin tension.

You can test for the best tension in stages. Sometimes a thread is fine enough for the needle but just a little too fragile to stitch out well. Winding it on the bobbin will make it easier to use. Loosening the tension screw may be all you need to do for these.

For threads that are just a little too thick or lumpy for the needle, simply putting the bobbin in the case upside down will straighten out the thread path and loosen the tension. This will work for most machines, except for those with asymmetrical bobbins.

For very thick threads, you may even want to bypass the bobbin tension system altogether. Instead of winding the thread through the usual pathway, just poke it out through the hole in the bobbin case. For drop-in bobbins, just ignore the tension path, and let the thread dangle.

Bypassing all tension systems with thicker threads

Rule 2: The thicker the thread, the longer the stitch.

Let the thread show its full glory. A short stitch length will chop the thread into itty bits. You also risk binding up the machine if you try to jam too much thread into tiny stitches. Instead, lengthen the stitch, and let the thread shine.

Remember, stitching out test samples does not waste thread—instead it uses the thread to get the machine set up properly. It *would* be a waste to mess up your project in order to save on thread.

Threads for the needle

We have one more aspect to consider. The thread you choose for the needle can add to the effect. Choose a thread that matches the fabric; then, tighten the needle tension just a little, and the bobbin thread will appear more segmented, giving the appearance of a row of beads.

See how matching needle thread to fabric makes bobbin thread look like beads?

Or, loosen the top tension and put a sexy thread in the needle. Your bobbin thread will stitch out to look like fine, hand-done couching. A metallic thread will give a snappy little flash of glitz.

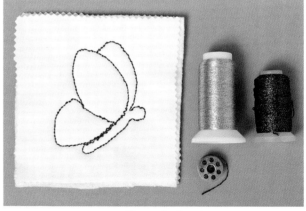

Metallic needle thread

Set aside time to play with thread combinations. When you find out how much fun it is, you may discover that bobbin work can be addicting.

midnight sunshine

Our next project for this chapter, *Midnight Sunshine*, makes use of satin stitches to decorate the urn and bobbin work to embellish the flower petals. We'll use the same basic technique for preparing the appliqués, but we'll use appliqué sheets instead of freezer paper. (For complete project instructions, see pages 60–64.)

The petals on the *Midnight Sunshine* flowers were bobbin worked with perle cotton in the bobbin (feed dogs engaged) after the petal edges were glue basted but before they were docked into the whole motif. The stitch length was set to stitch out about 8 stitches per inch. A shiny polyester thread (Highlights from Superior) was used in the needle, with the tension reduced so that the thread would show. And, of course, it was stitched with the stabilizer side up so that the fancy thread would show on the front.

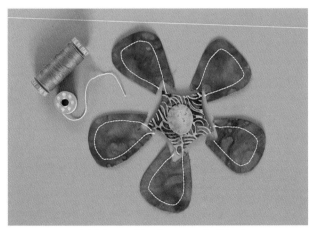

Midnight Sunshine flowers embellished
and ready for docking

DECORATE THE URN

Just for fun I decided that I wanted my urn to look as if it were faceted crystal. I chose a long oval satin stitch to reflect the shapes of cut glass. Simple lines of plain satin stitching near the upper and lower edges gave the look of a channel cut. The satin stitching was completed on the urn before the edges were glue basted. I used two layers of appliqué sheets to stabilize the urn for the decorative stitches.

Urn stitching detail

TUNNELING

Sometimes satin stitches can cause the fabric to draw up into the stitching line. Called tunneling, this distortion of fabric will result in messy, puckered shapes that just won't fit back together again. To prevent tunneling, you may need to stack up two or three layers of appliqué sheets. Be sure to stitch out the pattern on a fabric scrap backed with two layers before diving into the project piece.

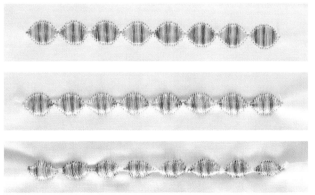

Examples of correct satin stitching (top)
and tunneling (middle and bottom rows).

AND THEN WE QUILT

The straight stitching on the urn, petals, and veins in the leaves are all free motion quilting lines. While free motion quilting takes practice to become skilled, it doesn't require nearly as much as you might think. Remember, anything worth doing is worth doing badly for as long as it takes.

The last step in my appliqué projects is my first step in quilting. The solid fabrics in our last project, *Wild Geraniums* (page 76), were chosen to let the quilting lines shine. I selected a thread that's a little showy and stitched in the ditch (the "under" edge) around the appliqué where the motifs meet the background. Using a thinner thread allows us to use a finer needle, resulting in a stitching line snuggled right up next to the turned edge of the appliqué. Stitching in the ditch around the appliqué defines the shapes, making them stand out from the background, and hides the appliqué stitching.

Detail of *Wild Geraniums* (page 76) shows a bobbin-work butterfly plus quilted petal and leaf veins.

My students often express surprise that I quilt within my appliqué shapes. Honestly, I didn't know there were rules about such things. Quilting lines add delicious dimension. My favorite quilting is adding detail to the shapes. I love stitching vein lines onto leaves!

As I finish each project I like to reflect on what was successful and what I might change. When you think of each quilt as practice for the next one, as I do, there are no mistakes or failures, just opportunities.

The Last Word: Done First

For some people, it seems that finishing is everything. At a weeklong quilting class many years ago, I shared a table with such a woman. We would be given an exercise to work on, and off she would go, pedal to the metal, roaring so fast that her machine shook our table.

If that wasn't disturbing enough, in just a few moments, she would yank her work out of the machine, wave it in the air above her head, and exclaim, "I'm done! I'm done!" Any concentration the rest of the class may have had was surely broken. Much muttering ensued.

Finally, after a day and a half of this, I had had enough. In my mind, I was looking for a way to ask her to cut it out that didn't start with "listen, wench." The next time she waved her work in the air, I found myself asking her why she was always in such a rush to be done. She confessed that it didn't really matter how well the work was done, it was important to her to be the first to finish. She didn't want to be last, which in her mind meant that she wasn't as talented as the rest of the students. We came to the understanding that she could just always be first and dispense with the announcement (which might make the slower people feel bad).

What I learned from her is that while some folks might consider quilting a competitive sport, we don't all play with the same goals. Done first does not necessarily mean done best. And besides, a perfect quilt may not have been fun to make.

If we rush to finish a quilt just to be done, we may not have learned all we need to know to do our best job. It's perfectly okay to let a project rest for a while.

It's also okay to decide not to finish a quilt. I mean, really, if we finish everything we start, there will be no quilt blocks for our grandchildren to discover in antiques shops.

When it comes to quilting, in my book, fun is better than finished any day.

ring o' posies

This darling wallhanging, designed to help you master basic hand appliqué by machine techniques, is just the right project to get you from appliqué novice to goddess! The pieced background, with its randomly placed color changes, gives our lovely appliqués the spiffy home they deserve.

FINISHED SIZE: about 23″ × 27½″   PIECED, APPLIQUÉD, AND QUILTED : by Beth Ferrier, 2008

materials

Yardage is based on 40"-wide fabric. Yardage amounts have been rounded up to include a little wiggle room. A fat quarter is 18" × 22".

- 1 fat quarter each of 3 similar fabrics for background

- 8–12 fat quarters or large scraps of fabric for appliqués. You will need light, medium, and dark fabrics in 2 colorways (yellow and purple in my quilt) for flower appliqués and light and dark green for the leaves.

- ½ yard fabric for appliqué circles, border accent, and binding

- ⅞ yard (27" × 32" rectangle) fabric for backing

- 27" × 32" piece of batting

- ¾" office dots (or use the circular template on page 41)

- 1 yard of freezer paper

cutting

FROM EACH BACKGROUND FABRIC

Cut 1 strip 5¾" × 22". Crosscut into 2 squares 5¾" × 5¾".

Cut 2 strips 5" × 22". Crosscut strips into 7 squares 5" × 5".

FROM THE BORDER ACCENT FABRIC

Cut 2 strips 3⅛" × width of fabric (WOF). Crosscut into 24 squares 3⅛" × 3⅛". Mark the diagonal on the wrong side of each square.

Cut 4 squares 2¾" × 2¾".

Cut 3 strips 2" × WOF for binding.

border block assembly

Unless otherwise noted, all pieced seam allowances are ¼".

MAKE THE FLYING GEESE UNITS

1. Place 2 border accent fabric 3⅛" × 3⅛" squares, right sides together, on opposite corners of a 5¾" × 5¾" background fabric square. The lines you drew on the wrong sides of the smaller squares should extend diagonally all the way across the larger square. And, yes, the smaller squares should overlap in the center.

2. Stitch ¼" from the line, on both sides of the line. Cut on the line, and press the seams toward the border accent fabric. Now you have 2 funny heart shapes.

Stitch on either side of line.   Press to form 2 heart shapes.

3. Place another border accent fabric square, right sides together, on each heart shape so that the line extends from the remaining corner and between the 2 triangles. Stitch ¼" from the line on both sides of the line.

Goose trick, step 3

4. Cut on the lines, and press the seams toward the border accent fabric. Ta-da! Too cool, huh?

Flying Geese unit

5. Repeat Steps 1–4 with the rest of the 5¾″ × 5¾″ background fabric squares and the remaining 3⅛″ × 3⅛″ border fabric squares. Each Flying Geese Unit should measure 2¾″ × 5″. We're making 24, but you only need 18 to finish the quilt top. The extra units will give you an assortment to choose from.

CREATE THE BORDER STRIPS

1. For the top and bottom borders, sew 4 Flying Geese units together. Press. Add a 2¾″ × 2¾″ accent fabric square to each end. Press. Make 2.

Top and bottom borders

2. For the side borders, sew 5 Flying Geese blocks together. Press. Make 2.

Side borders

make the background

1. Lay out the 5″ × 5″ background squares into a 4 × 5 grid, and arrange the fabrics in a pleasing order. For this quilt, the goal is to spread the fabrics evenly around the background.

2. Sew the squares into rows, pressing the seams so they will fit neatly together when you sew the rows together.

add the borders

1. Add the side border strips to the pieced center and press.

2. Add the top and bottom borders. Press very carefully to prepare for the appliqué.

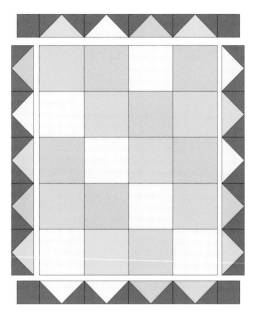

Background Assembly Diagram

make the appliqués

1. Make the appliqués as described in Chapter 1 on pages 4–12, using the templates on page 41. (A template for the berries is provided if you don't want to use office dots.) Refer to the project photo for placement guidance, or invent your own arrangement.

2. Dock and stitch appliqués together.

3. Sew appliqué motifs to the background as described on pages 13–14.

finishing

Use your favorite method to quilt, bind, and finish the quilt.

A

B

F

G

Flower
Make 6.

C

E

D

Leaf
Make 5 as is and
5 reversed.

Berry
Make 13.

Ring O' Posies

still life

For centuries the still life has been the favorite subject for artists as they perfect their skills. Now it's your turn to play. I've created two versions of this quilt. The batik quilt above uses simple shapes to show basic shading. The second quilt shows how a few extra cuts can add depth and dimension to a simple design. The directions here are for the simpler design. Refer to pages 19–20 for detailed instructions for the more complex design.

FINISHED SIZE: about 16″ × 20″ · · · · · · · **PIECED, APPLIQUÉD, AND QUILTED** | by Beth Ferrier, 2008

materials

Yardage is based on 40″-wide fabric. Yardage amounts have been rounded up to include a little wiggle room. A fat quarter is 18″ × 22″. A fat eighth is 9″ × 22″.

- 1 fat quarter of fabric for a simple background *or* several large scraps for a pieced background

- 12–15 fat eighths or large scraps of fabric in several shades of pear, apple, stem, and leaf colors for appliqués

- 1 fat quarter of fabric for binding

- ⅝ yard fabric for backing

- 20″ × 24″ piece of batting

- 1 yard of freezer paper

 # cutting

FROM THE BACKGROUND FABRIC

Cut 1 rectangle 16″ × 20″.

FROM THE BACKING FABRIC

Cut 1 rectangle 20″ × 24″.

FROM THE BINDING FABRIC

Cut 5 strips 2″ × 22″.

 # make the appliqués

1. Make the appliqués as described in Chapter 2 on pages 16–18, using the templates on pages 44–47.

2. Dock and stitch the appliqués together.

3. Place the completed appliqué as desired on the background fabric, and stitch in place as described on pages 13–14.

 # finishing

Use your favorite method to quilt, bind, and finish the quilt.

complex design

Subdivide the appliqué shapes in any way; the sample appliqué design shown here is just one suggestion. Use additional scraps or fat eighths for more shading options.

Sample appliqué design

Note how subdividing our basic shapes makes the appliqué more interesting.

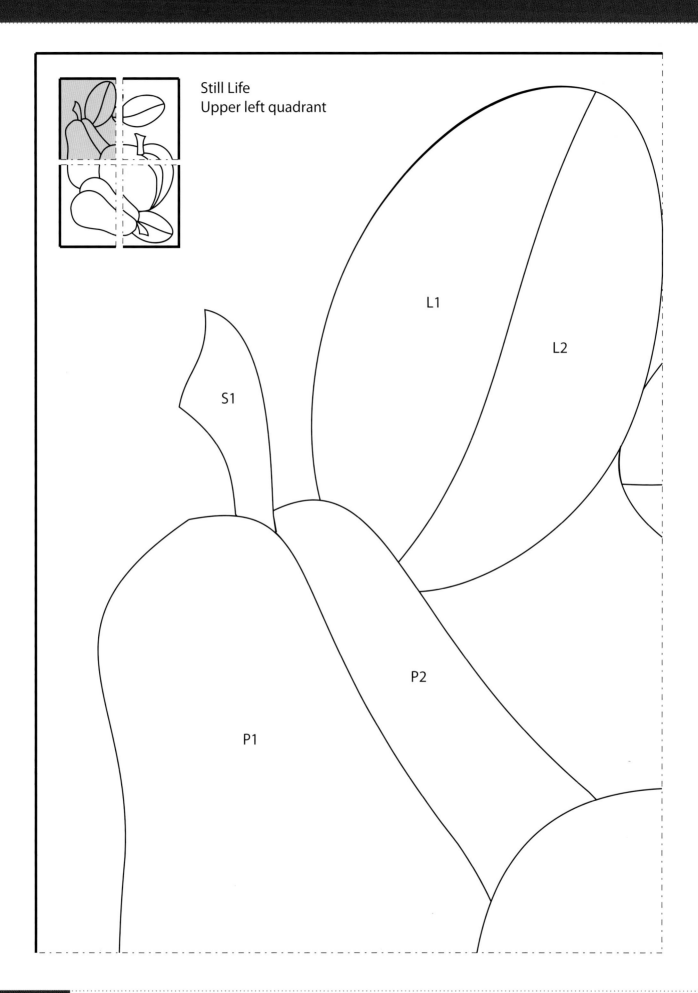

Still Life
Upper left quadrant

L1

L2

S1

P2

P1

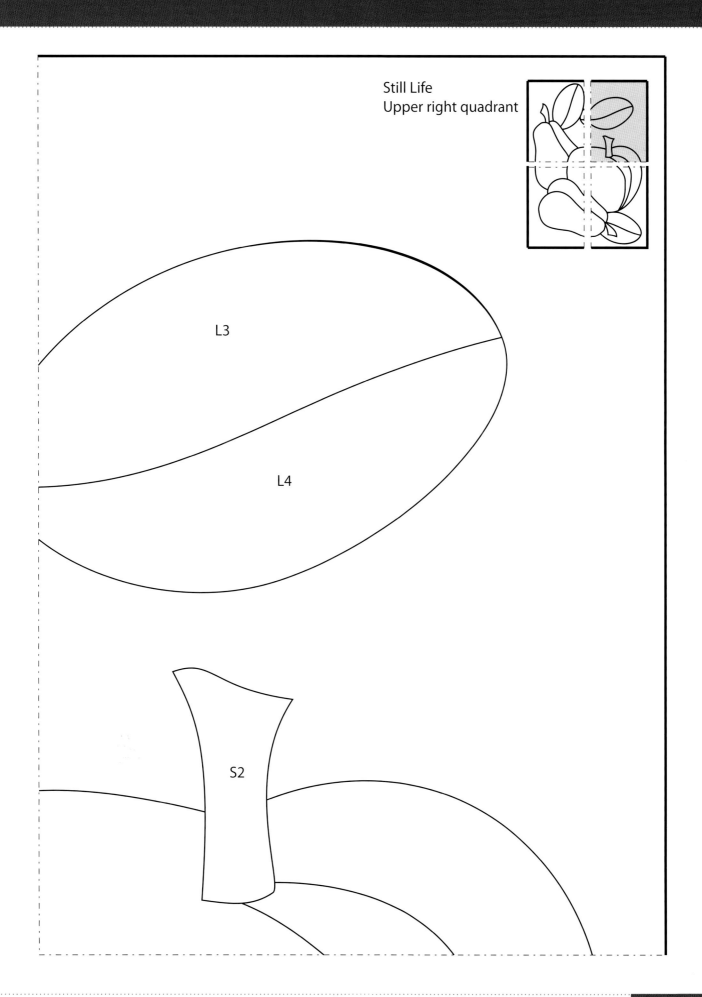

Still Life
Upper right quadrant

L3

L4

S2

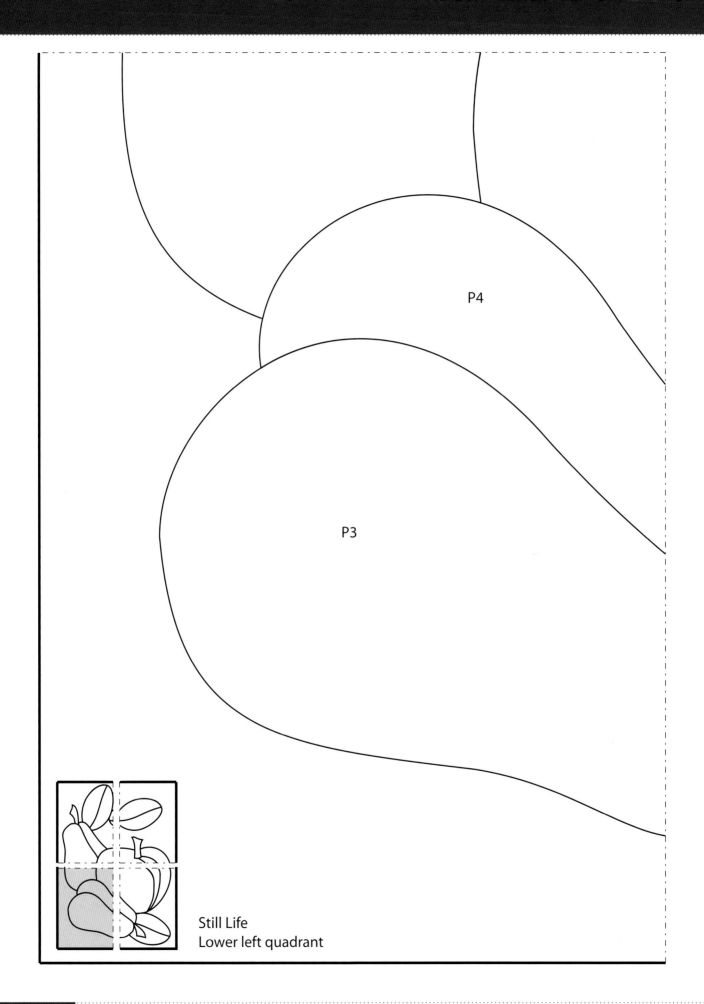

P4

P3

Still Life
Lower left quadrant

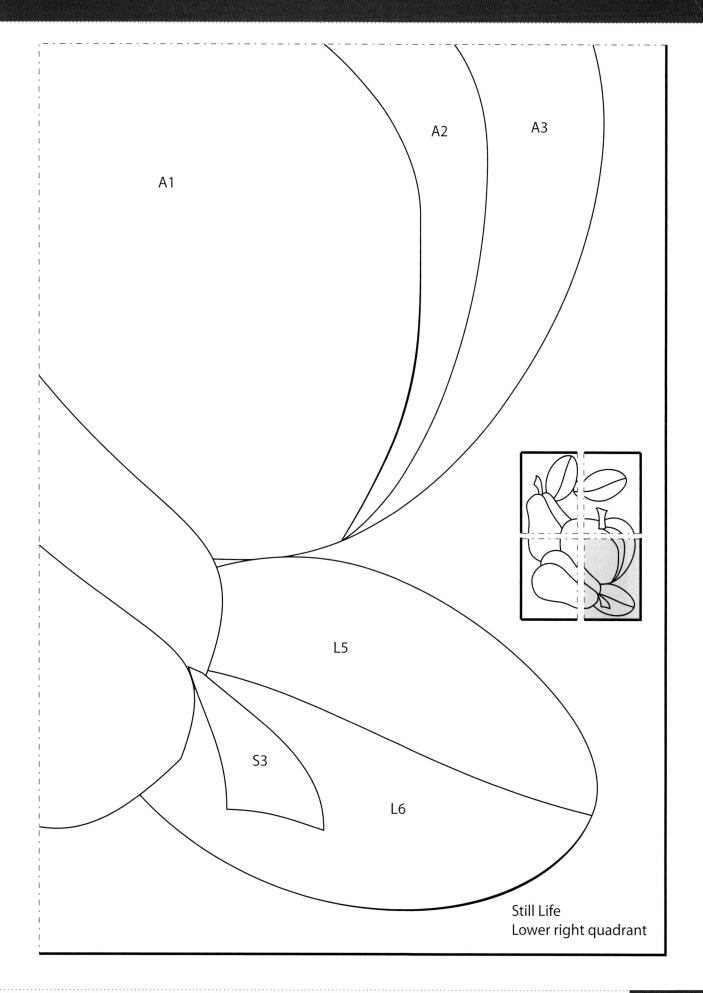

A1

A2

A3

L5

S3

L6

Still Life
Lower right quadrant

coxcomb quadrille

While red and green are my favorite colors, and I think every quilt should include them, imagine how charming this quilt would be in pinks or blues—or both! A really beautiful quilt will draw us in. The trapuntoed flowers, softly shaded background fabrics, and dense quilting pattern take turns catching our attention. It's the small details that make the quilt more interesting.

FINISHED SIZE: about 38½″ × 38½″   PIECED, APPLIQUÉD, AND QUILTED   by Beth Ferrier, 2008

 materials

Yardage is based on 40"-wide fabric unless noted. Yardage amounts have been rounded up to include a little wiggle room. A fat quarter is 18" × 22".

note

The suggested amounts are totals; I used little bits of lots of fabrics for my quilt.

- ⅓ yard each of 6 different fabrics for the background (includes the binding)

- 2–3 fat quarters of green fabric for leaf and stem appliqués

- 3–4 fat quarters of red fabric for flower appliqués

- 1 fat quarter of yellow fabric for flower center appliqués

- 42" × 42" square (1¼ yards) of fabric for backing. Use a 42"-wide fabric or piece, if necessary.

- 12 sheets of C&T Wash-Away Appliqué Sheets

- Craft-size package of Soft & Bright batting for trapunto padding

- 42" × 42" square of batting

 cutting

FROM EACH BACKGROUND FABRIC

Cut 1 strip 4½" × WOF. Crosscut into 6 squares 4½" × 4½" and 5 rectangles 2½" × 4½".

Cut 2 strips 2½" × WOF. Crosscut into 9 rectangles 2½" × 4½" and 9 squares 2½" × 2½".

Cut 1 strip 2" × WOF for binding

FROM THE STEM FABRIC

Cut 8 bias strips 1" × 10" and 2 bias strips 1" × 18" for stems

 make the background

Unless otherwise noted, all pieced seam allowances are ¹⁄₄".

1. Begin by making the uneven four-patches. Use the fabric randomly. My only rule is to avoid sewing the same fabrics together. Make 25.

Uneven four-patch

2. Similarly, make the blocks for the edges of the quilt. These are the A blocks that will line the bottom and right edge of the quilt. Make 10.

Block A

3. Make an uneven nine-patch (the B block) for the lower right corner of the background.

Block B

4. Sew together the basic block units to make bigger blocks. Start by sewing together 4 uneven Four-Patch blocks to make bigger four-patches. Make 4.

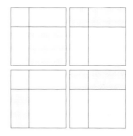

Bigger four-patch units

5. Use 2 basic blocks and 2 A blocks to make four-patches for the right edge of the quilt. Make 2.

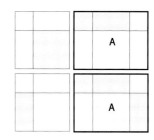

Right edge blocks

6. Repeat step 5, placing the A block below the basic block, for the bottom row of the quilt. These really are different! Make 2.

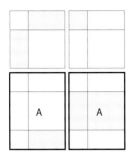

Bottom edge blocks

7. Make one last special unit for the lower right corner using 1 four-patch unit, 2 A's, and a B block. Just make one.

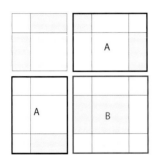

Lower right corner block

8. Now you just have one big nine-patch to put together for the background. Press the piece thoroughly. This is a perfect time to use spray sizing (I prefer the brand Magic Sizing) to make the piece super flat, which will make it easier to appliqué.

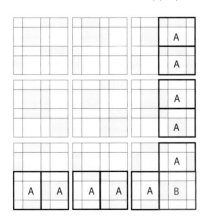

Background Assembly Diagram

make the appliqués

1. Make the trapunto flower appliqués as described on pages 20–22. Use the appliqué sheets to make the flower templates (page 51), but make them the same way you would if you were using freezer paper. Stack 6 layers of the appliqué sheets, shiny sides facing up, and staple the templates in place.

2. For the trapunto batting for the flowers, make a template from a scrap of fabric. Remember to cut it slightly smaller than the whole outline of the flower. Make 12 batting shapes. The leaves in my quilt are not trapuntoed, but you can trapunto yours if you like.

3. Make 12 coxcomb flower appliqués with batting.

4. Make 24 leaf appliqués (12 and 12 reversed) without batting.

MAKE THE STEMS

1. Cut 1" bias strips for the stems. Fold and press them in thirds, wrong sides together, as described on page 12. Spray sizing makes crisp edges, which are easier to stitch down.

2. Make 8 strips 10" long and 2 strips 18" long. If needed, sew shorter lengths together to make the longer strips. Sew the strips together on the diagonal (just as we would to create our bindings), pressing the seams open.

SEW ON THE APPLIQUÉS

Place the motifs as desired on the pieced background. Use flat flower-head pins to hold the motifs in place, and stitch them down as described on page 13–14.

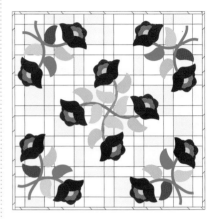

Suggested placement diagram

finishing

Use your favorite method to quilt, bind, and finish the quilt.

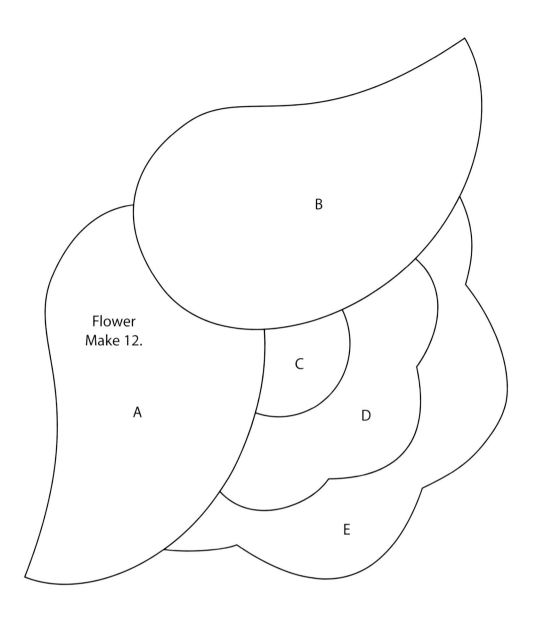

Flower
Make 12.

A

B

C

D

E

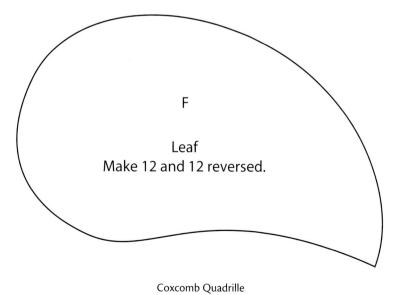

F

Leaf
Make 12 and 12 reversed.

Coxcomb Quadrille

carnations, anyone?

With this lovely vase of flowers, your thread stash can finally step up and be seen. What? No thread stash? This quilt can be a perfect excuse to start collecting today. Have fun with these cheerful flowers. Instead of careful planning, random fabric placement gives the bouquet its happy zing.

FINISHED SIZE: about 21½″ × 25½″   **PIECED, APPLIQUÉD, AND QUILTED** : by Beth Ferrier, 2008

 materials

Yardage is based on 40"-wide fabric. Yardage amounts have been rounded up to include a little wiggle room. A fat quarter is 18" × 22".

- ½ yard of fabric for background

- Fat quarters or large scraps for appliqué in:

    5 values of pink flower colors—light, light medium, medium, dark medium, and dark

    2–3 values of green leaf colors

    2–3 values of beige for vase and baby's breath flowers

- ¼ yard of fabric for background accent

- ¼ yard of fabric for binding*

- 26" × 30" rectangle (¾ yard) of fabric for backing

- 26" × 30" piece of batting

- 1 yard of freezer paper

 cutting

FROM THE BACKGROUND FABRIC A

Cut 1 strip 9" × WOF. Cut 1 segment 9" × 25½". Cut the remainder of the strip into 3 strips each 3" wide (3" × 16½" each).

Cut 1 strip 5½" × WOF. Crosscut into 1 segment 5½" × 25½".

FROM THE BACKGROUND ACCENT FABRIC B

Cut 2 strips 3" × WOF. Crosscut into 3 strips 3" × 16½".

FROM THE BINDING FABRIC

Cut 3 strips 2" × WOF for the binding.*

* *Note:* My fabric was very cleverly designed with the stripes printed on the diagonal. To achieve the same look with traditionally striped fabric, you'll need to cut strips on the bias. A fat quarter would require fewer seams than a straight quarter.

 make the background

Unless otherwise noted, all pieced seam allowances are ¼".

1. Begin with the 3" background and background accent fabric strips. Make 2 different strip sets by joining their long edges as follows:

A. Accent-Background-Accent for the dark strip set

Strip set 1

B. Background-Accent-Background for the light strip set

Strip set 2

2. Press the seams toward the darker fabric. Crosscut each strip set into five 3" segments.

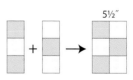

3. Assemble these strip set segments into 5 six-pack units. Press.

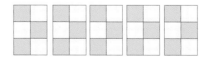

Six packs

4. Assemble the checkerboard panel by joining 5 six-pack units as shown. Press.

Strip of six packs

5. Sew the background strips to each side of the checkerboard strip, with the 5½" × 25½" strip on the left and the 9" × 25½" strip on the right. Pressing the seams toward the pieced strip will make the accent squares float instead of recede.

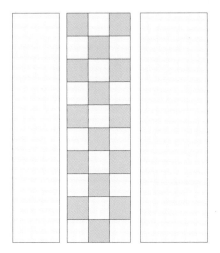

Background Assembly Diagram

 make the appliqués

1. Make the appliqués as described on pages 4–12, using the templates on page 54–55. Make 6 carnations, 11 leaves, 12 baby's breath, and 1 vase. The fun and funky flower shapes provide lots of opportunity to play with color and value placement.

2. Use matching or contrasting thread to stitch the parts together to create the desired effect. Real live carnations have a lovely raggedy edge. Suggest that in your project by using contrasting threads and a zigzag stitch. See Chapter 4, page 29–37, for ideas. The look can be as subtle (small contrast and fine threads) or dramatic (lots of contrast and a thicker thread) as your heart desires. Stitch the appliqués to the background using the project photos as a guide.

 finishing

Use your favorite method to quilt, bind, and finish the quilt.

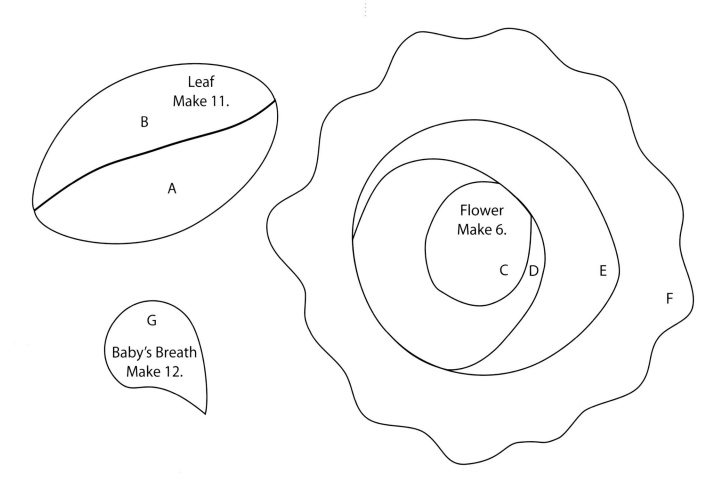

Leaf
Make 11.

B

A

G

Baby's Breath
Make 12.

Flower
Make 6.

C D

E

F

Carnations, Anyone?

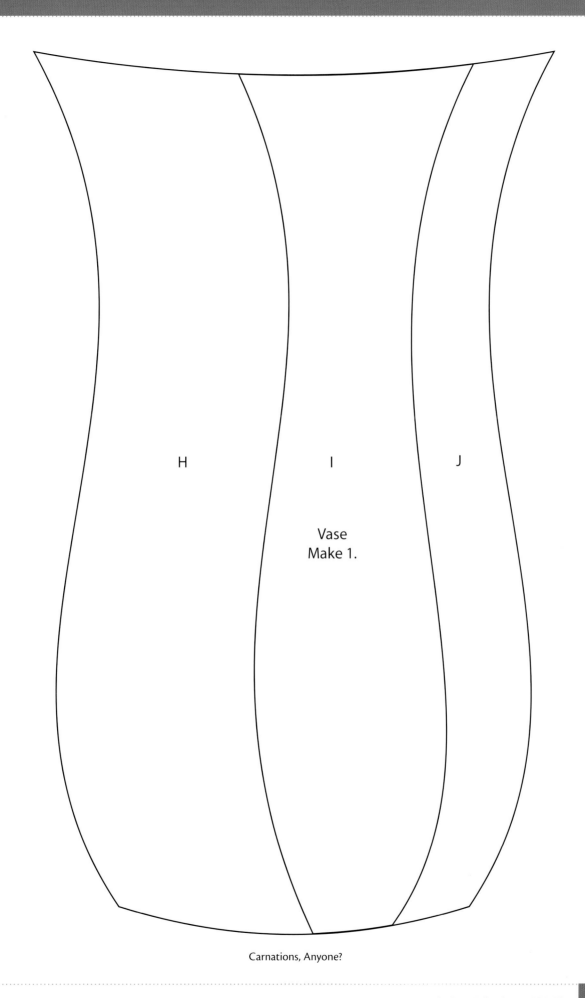

H   I   J

Vase
Make 1.

Carnations, Anyone?

Victorian Cat

Hey, kitty, kitty, kitty! Make yours mod or retro, cool or country (shown on next page). At last, a cat with spots where we want them! Let's play with thread, stitches, and shapes as we create our pets and then finish by surrounding our kitten with cozy (or crazy) quilting.

FINISHED SIZE: about 18″ × 18″   **PIECED, APPLIQUÉD, AND QUILTED** by Beth Ferrier, 2008

# materials

Yardage is based on 40″-wide fabric. Yardage amounts have been rounded up to include a little wiggle room. A fat quarter is 18″ × 22″.

This is what I used for each of my renditions of the *Calico Cat*:

Victorian Cat

- 8–9 fat quarters of several fabrics for the body (I used Cherrywood hand-dyed fabric.)
- Variety of polyester, rayon, and metallic threads for decorative stitching

Groovy Kitty

- 1 fat quarter of fabric for main body
- Scraps of fabrics for other body parts
- Black thread (Bottom Line Superior or Deco Bob WonderFil) for decorative stitching

Country Kitten

- Fabric collection of 10″ × 10″ squares (I used Moda Fabric) for the body
- Rayon thread by Presencia for decorative stitching

And, to make each cat

- 1 fat quarter or 18″ × 18″ square of fabric for background
- 1 fat quarter of fabric for binding
- 22″ × 22″ square of fabric for backing
- 22″ × 22″ square of batting
- 4 sheets of C&T Wash-Away Appliqué Sheets

# cutting

FROM THE BINDING FABRIC

Cut 5 strips 2″ × 22″.

# create the templates

1. Make 2 copies of the templates (pages 58–59). Glue or tape the pattern sections together to make 2 complete diagrams. Set aside one for the Key.

2. Staple one template to 2 layers of appliqué sheets, with both layers shiny side up. Cut apart the sections, and place them on the Key.

make the appliqués

Make the appliqués as described on pages 16–18, using the templates and the appliqué sheets. For the *Victorian Cat*, add decorative stitching to the sections before basting and docking as described in Chapter 4 (pages 33–34). For the other two cats, dock and baste first, following the basic instructions. Then add the decorative stitching. Complete all the decorative stitching before stitching the kitties to the background.

finishing

Use your favorite method to quilt, bind, and finish the quilt.

Groovy Kitty

Country Kitten

Top half

Calico Cat

Bottom half

Calico Cat

midnight sunshine

Rich colors and a nifty border treatment nicely focus our attention on the decorated appliqué. We can be either dramatic or playful just by changing the type of thread used in the bobbin-worked flowers and the urn, embellished with machine embroidery.

FINISHED SIZE: about 25½" × 29½"   **PIECED, APPLIQUÉD, AND QUILTED**   by Beth Ferrier, 2008

 materials

Yardage is based on 40″-wide fabric. Yardage amounts have been rounded up to include a little wiggle room. A fat quarter is 18″ × 22″. A fat eighth is 9″ × 22″.

- 1 yard of dark fabric for the background and border
- ⅓ yard of light fabric for border
- 1 fat eighth each of 5 fabrics for flower appliqués
- 1 fat eighth or scraps of medium green fabric for leaf appliqués
- 1 fat eighth or scraps of light green fabric for leaf appliqués
- 1 fat eighth or scraps of fabric for berry appliqués
- ⅝ yard of fabric for vase appliqué, accent strips, and binding
- 30″ × 34″ rectangle (⅞ yard) of fabric for backing
- 30″ × 34″ piece of batting
- Perle cotton or decorative thread for decorative stitching
- 8 sheets of C&T Wash-Away Appliqué Sheets
- 1″ office dots as an alternative to the berry template

 cutting

FROM THE DARK BACKGROUND/BORDER FABRIC

Cut 1 rectangle 20½″ × 24½″ for the appliqué background.

Cut 2 strips 3″ × WOF. From these strips cut:

  1 rectangle 3″ × 12½″ for the top border.

  1 rectangle 3″ × 12″ for the bottom border.

  1 rectangle 3″ × 10½″ for the left border.

  1 rectangle 3″ × 8″ for the right border.

FROM THE LIGHT BORDER FABRIC

Cut 2 strips 3″ × WOF. From these strips cut:

  1 rectangle 3″ × 18″ for the left border.

  1 rectangle 3″ × 17″ for the top border.

  1 rectangle 3″ × 17½″ for the bottom border.

  1 rectangle 3″ × 20½″ for the right border.

FROM THE VASE, ACCENT STRIP, AND BINDING FABRIC

Cut 4 strips ¾″ × WOF for the accent strips.

Cut 4 strips 2″ × WOF for the binding

make the appliqués

Who wants to mess with a bigger piece of fabric if it's not needed? Not me! Let's complete the appliqué first, before adding all the borders.

1. From the appliqué sheets, cut out the templates (pages 63–64) for 1 large flower, 3 full flowers, and 3 profile flowers. Also cut out appliqué sheet templates for 9 leaves, 10 berries, and 2 urns.

2. Prepare the flower appliqués up to the docking stage. Following the instructions on pages 34–36, load the perle cotton onto a bobbin. Loosen the bobbin tension, or bypass the tension if necessary. Lengthen the stitch. Working slowly, stitch each petal, stabilizer side up, to embellish it. Dock and stitch the flowers together.

3. Press one appliqué sheet urn to the wrong side of the desired fabric. Carefully align the second appliqué urn template with the first and press. Using decorative threads, embellish the urn as desired. See page 36 for suggested stitching patterns.

4. Using the project photo as a guide, place the completed appliqués, and stitch them to the 20½″ × 24½″ background fabric rectangle.

make the accent strips and border

Unless otherwise noted, all pieced seam allowances are ¼".

MAKE THE ACCENT STRIPS

1. Press the ¾" accent strips in half lengthwise, wrong sides together, just as you would press a binding strip.

2. Machine baste these strips to the edge of the appliquéd background fabric rectangle. Baste them to the short sides first. Trim to fit. Stitch to the long sides next, overlapping in the corners.

CREATE THE BORDERS

1. Dig out the strips that you cut for the left border. Overlap the strips at right angles, right sides together. To get the angles to come out correctly, the fabrics must be oriented as they are in the diagram. Trim the selvages, or offset the strips so that the selvages will be cut away.

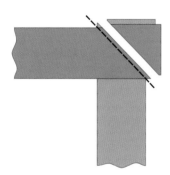

Side border seams

2. Sew from upper left to lower right. This direction really matters to ensure that you get the angle going in the correct direction. Trim the excess, leaving a ¼" seam allowance. Press the seam toward the light fabric.

3. Pin the border strip to the left side of the appliquéd rectangle. (There is a little wiggle room in the length of the pieced border strips.) Position as desired. Trim and pin in place.

4. Repeat this process for the right border.

5. Sew the side borders in place. Press the seam toward the borders. Press the accent strip toward the appliqué background rectangle.

6. For the top and bottom border, the process is essentially the same *except* for the way the strips are turned for sewing. Yes, it really is different, and it really does matter. Sew the top and bottom borders in place and trim.

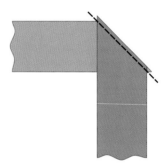

Top and bottom border seams

finishing

Use your favorite method to quilt, bind, and finish the quilt.

A

B

G

F

C

Large Flower
Make 1.

E

D

N

J

M

I

H

K

Medium Flower
Make 2 and
1 reversed.

L

Midnight Sunshine

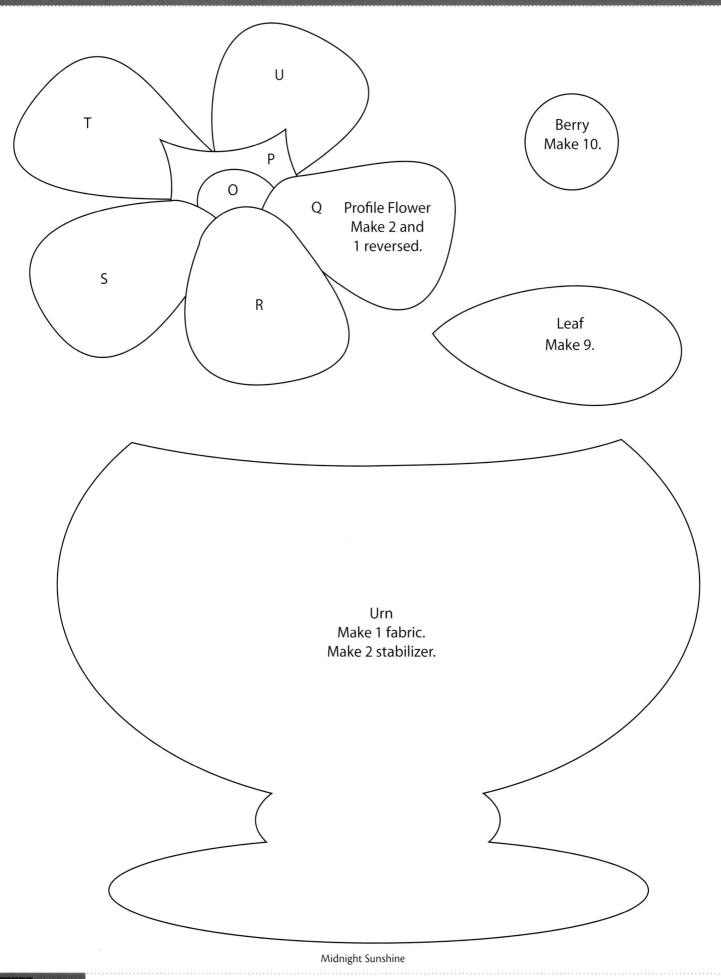

T

U

P

O

Q Profile Flower
Make 2 and
1 reversed.

S

R

Berry
Make 10.

Leaf
Make 9.

Urn
Make 1 fabric.
Make 2 stabilizer.

Midnight Sunshine

saginaw sunflowers

What could be more charming than a pail of sunflowers? This project is perfect for using up those little bits of yellow left over from other projects. Why stick to just a few fabrics when we could use so many more!

FINISHED SIZE: about 25″ × 31½″   PIECED, APPLIQUÉD, AND QUILTED by Beth Ferrier, 2008.

# materials

Yardage is based on 40"-wide fabric. Yardage amounts have been rounded up to include a little wiggle room. A fat quarter is 18" × 22". A fat eighth is 9" × 22".

- ⅝ yard of light fabric for sky
- 1 fat eighth of fabric for dark sky
- ⅛ yard of white fabric for background accent
- 1 fat quarter of fabric for light grass
- 1 fat quarter of fabric for dark grass
- 1 fat quarter of green fabric for stems
- 1 fat eighth each of 5 shades of yellow fabric for flower petal appliqués
- 1 fat eighth of brown fabric or 5 scraps for flower center appliqués
- 1 fat eighth each or scraps of 2 shades of green fabric for leaf appliqués
- 1 fat eighth each or scraps of 4 shades of gray fabric for pail appliqué
- Scraps of black and other fabrics for butterfly appliqués
- ¼ yard of fabric for binding*
- 29" × 36" rectangle (⅞ yard) of fabric for backing
- 29" × 36" piece of batting
- 2 yards of freezer paper

# cutting

FROM THE LIGHT SKY FABRIC

Cut 1 rectangle 19" × 21½", and label it "A."

FROM THE DARK SKY FABRIC

Cut 1 rectangle 5½" × 21½", and label it "B."

FROM THE WHITE BACKGROUND ACCENT FABRIC

Cut 2 strips 1½" × WOF. Crosscut into 1 segment 1½" × 26½", 1 segment 1½" × 4½", and 1 segment 1½" × 25½".

FROM THE LIGHT GRASS FABRIC

Cut 1 rectangle 19" × 5½", and label it "C."

Cut 1 rectangle 5½" × 4½", and label it "D."

FROM THE DARK GRASS FABRIC

Cut 1 rectangle 19" × 4½", and label it "E."

Cut 1 square 5½" × 5½", and label it "F."

FROM THE STEM FABRIC

Cut 4 bias strips 1" × 10".

FROM THE BINDING FABRIC

Cut 3 strips 2" × WOF.*

* *Note:* If you're using a striped fabric for the binding, consider cutting it on the bias as I did for my quilt. A fat quarter would require fewer seams than a straight quarter.

# make the background

Unless otherwise noted, all pieced seam allowances are ¼".

1. Sew the light grass fabric rectangle C to the light sky fabric rectangle A. Press the seam toward C.

2. Sew the dark grass square F to the dark sky fabric rectangle B. Press this seam toward F.

3. Sew a 1½" × 26½" white background accent strip to the right edge of the A/C unit. All seams are pressed toward the white background accent strips.

4. Sew the B/F unit to the background accent strip. Press.

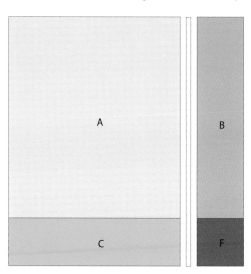

A/C unit plus B/F unit

5. Sew the 1½″ × 4½″ white background accent strip to the right 4½″ edge of the grass fabric rectangle E. Press. Sew the remaining light grass fabric rectangle D to the white background accent strip. Press.

E/D unit

6. Sew the 1½″ × 25½″ white background accent strip to the top edge of the E/D unit. Press.

Add background accent to E/D unit

7. Sew the E/D unit from Step 6 to the A/C/B/F unit from Step 4. Press well. Time to appliqué!

Ta-da! It's a background.

make the appliqués

1. Press the stem fabric bias strips into thirds lengthwise (see page 12) to form the stems.

2. Following the basic instructions for appliqué (pages 4–12) and the color suggestions on pages 23–26, prepare the flower and leaf appliqué templates (pages 68–70).

3. Stitch the finished appliqués to the background as described on pages 13–14.

finishing

Use your favorite method to quilt, bind, and finish the quilt.

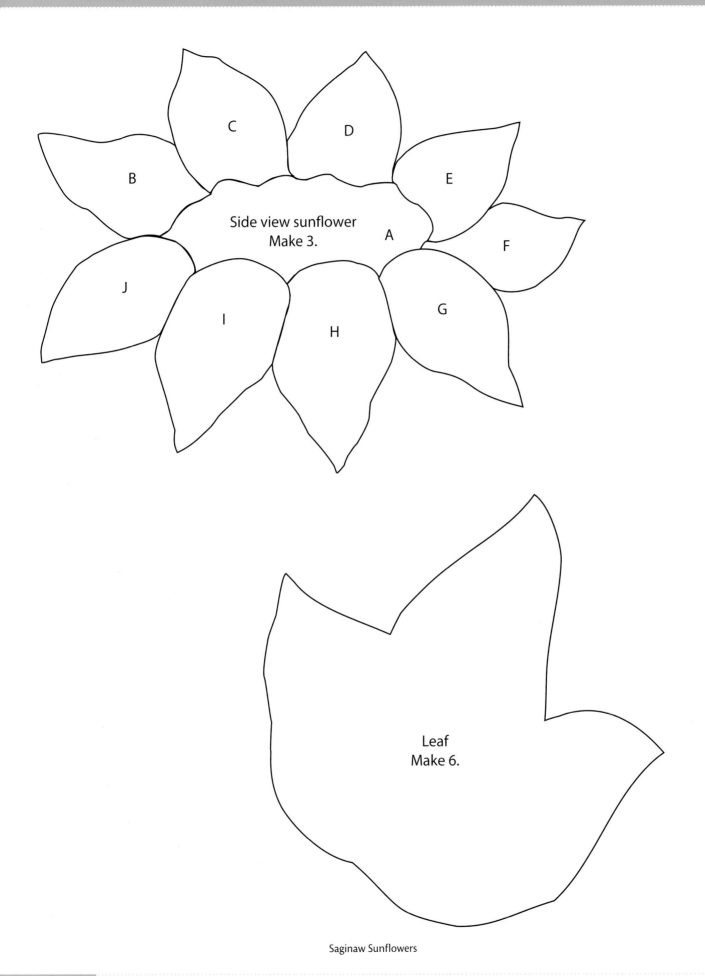

Side view sunflower
Make 3.

B

C

D

E

F

A

J

I

H

G

Leaf
Make 6.

Saginaw Sunflowers

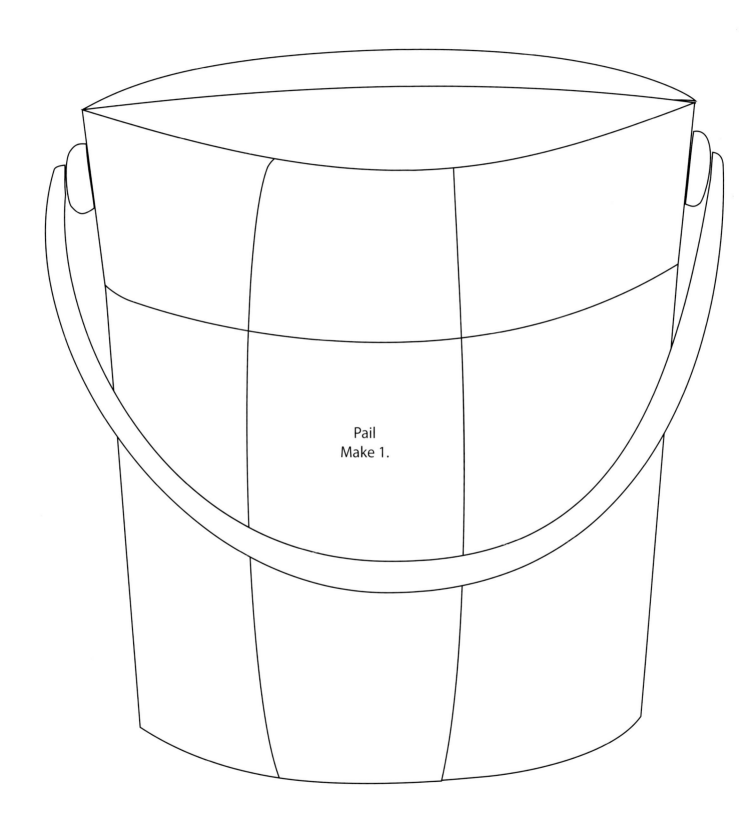

Pail
Make 1.

Saginaw Sunflowers

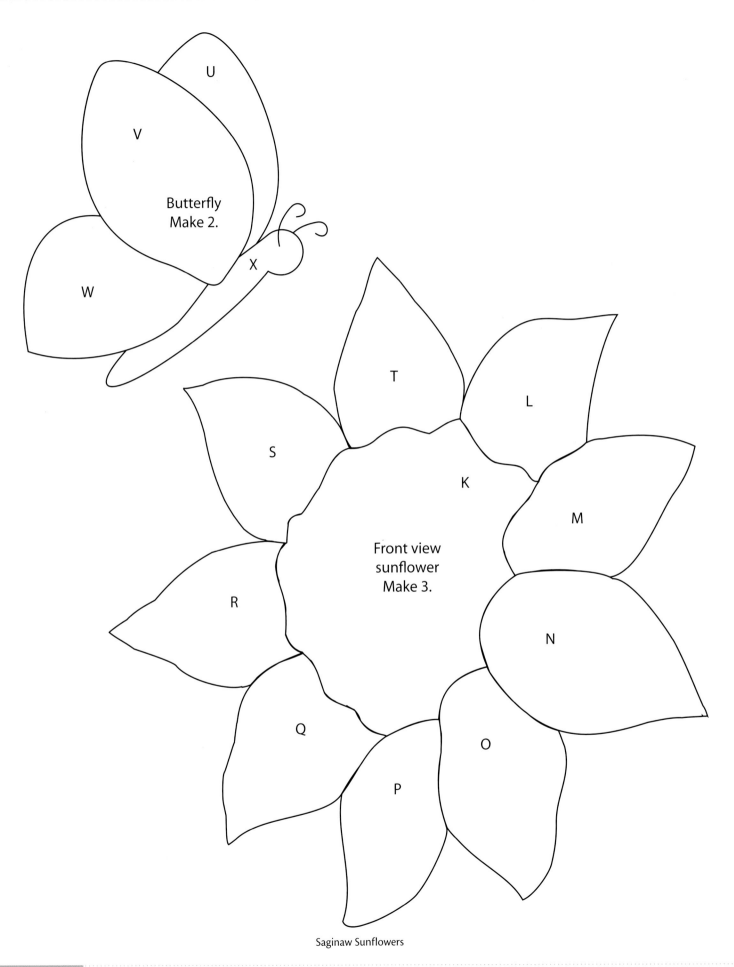

U

V

Butterfly
Make 2.

X

W

T

L

S

K

M

Front view
sunflower
Make 3.

R

N

Q

O

P

Saginaw Sunflowers

rose garland

Civil War Rose Garland

This wallhanging is just the right size to hang above a door or spread across a buffet. Stitch it up in your favorite fabric style. Here, I offer in three versions—cozy country, bright color (page 72), and elegant silks (page 73).

FINISHED SIZE: about 30½″ × 13½″   **PIECED, APPLIQUÉD, AND QUILTED** by Beth Ferrier, 2008

Brights Rose Garland

 materials

Yardage is based on 40″-wide fabric. Yardage amounts have been rounded up to include a little wiggle room. A fat quarter is 18″ × 22″. A fat eighth is 9″ × 22″.

- Fat quarters or large scraps of several flower and leaf fabrics for appliqués

- ½ yard of beige fabric (or 1 yard of Dupioni silk) for background

- ⅓ yard of dark brown fabric for inner accent border

- 18″ × 35″ rectangle (½ yard) of fabric for backing

- 18″ × 35″ piece of batting

- 1 yard of freezer paper

 cutting

FROM THE BACKGROUND FABRIC

Cut 1 rectangle 9½″ × 26½″ (cut silk along the *length* of the fabric to have the slubs run vertically).

Cut 1 strip 1½″ × WOF for the inner accent borders.

Cut 3 strips 2″ × WOF. Crosscut 2 rectangles 2″ × 10½″ from a strip for the side outer borders. Trim the remaining strips to 2″ × 30½″ for the top and bottom outer borders.

FROM THE DARK BROWN ACCENT FABRIC

Cut 1 strip 1½″ × WOF for the inner accent border.

Cut 3 strips 2″ × WOF for the binding.

 make the background accent strip

Unless otherwise noted, all pieced seam allowances are ¼″.

1. Along the length of the strips, sew the 1½″ background fabric and accent fabric strips right sides together. Always press the seams toward the accent fabric.

Sew strips together.

2. Cut the strip set from Step 1 in half. Sew the halves together. Press the seam toward the accent fabric.

Sew halves together.

3. Cut the strip set from Step 2 into 18 segments each 1″ wide.

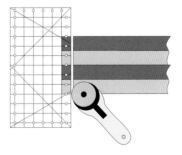

Cut into segments.

Silk Rose Garland

4. Set aside 2 of the segments from Step 3. Sew the rest together in pairs, end to end, to form 8 longer segments. Press.

Make 8 longer segments.

5. For the side accent strips, you need a background fabric rectangle at both ends of the strip. Unsew the background fabric rectangles from the ends of the 2 remaining little segments from Step 4. Don't throw them away!

Unsew background rectangles.

6. Sew the 2 unsewn rectangles to the ends of 2 of the longer segments from Step 4 to form the side accent strips. Press.

Sew background rectangle to end.

7. For each top and bottom accent strip, sew 3 longer segments from Step 4 together, end to end. Add the segments that you took the background fabric rectangles from to the one end of each of these strips to complete the top and bottom borders. Press.

Additional segment

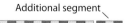

Top and bottom accent strips

8. Sew the side accent strips to the 9½" sides of the background rectangle. Press the seams toward the accent strip.

(Spray sizing helps.) Sew the top and bottom accent strips in place. Press.

add the plain borders

Sew the side borders on first, pressing toward the inner accent border, and then add the top and bottom borders. Press.

Background Assembly Diagram

make the appliqués

1. Make the appliqués as described on pages 4–12, using the templates on pages 74–75. Freezer paper works just fine for this project.

2. Stitch the appliqués onto the background as described on pages 13–14.

finishing

Use your favorite method to quilt, bind, and finish the quilt.

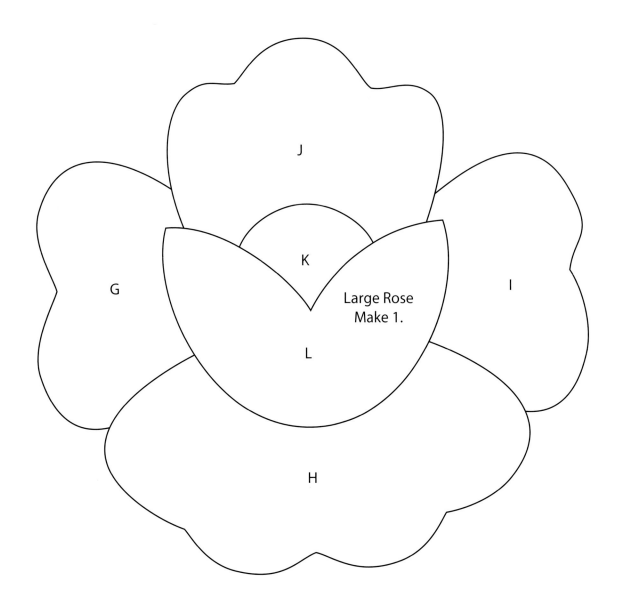

J

K

G

Large Rose
Make 1.

I

L

H

Rose Garland

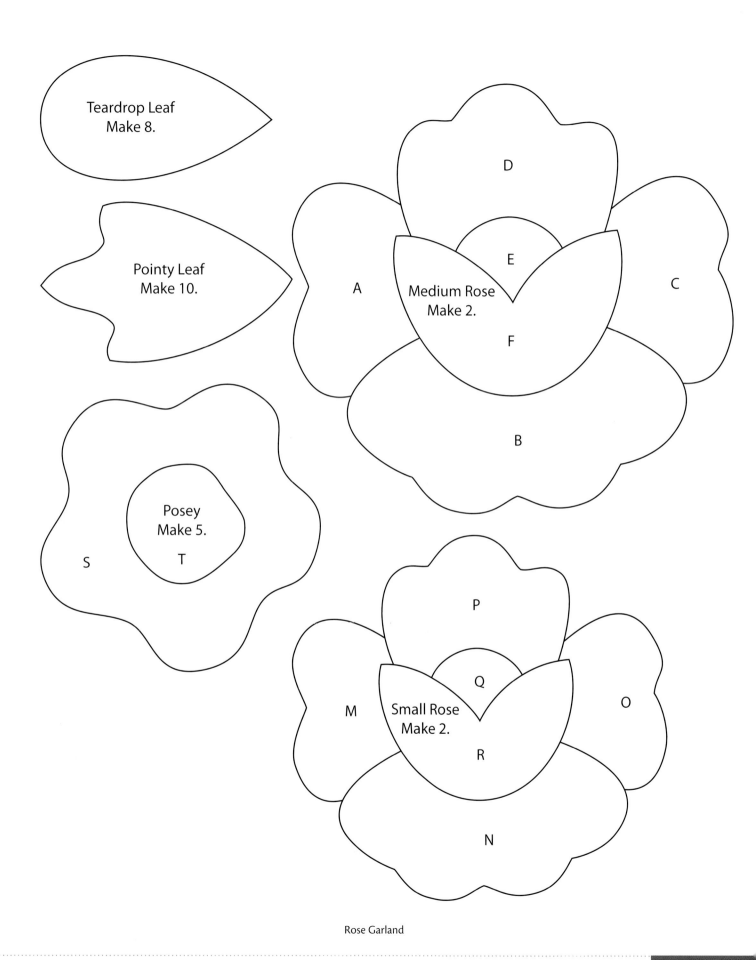

Teardrop Leaf
Make 8.

Pointy Leaf
Make 10.

D

E

A

Medium Rose
Make 2.

C

F

B

Posey
Make 5.

S

T

P

Q

M

Small Rose
Make 2.

O

R

N

Rose Garland

As appliquérs, our focus is usually on finding the perfect fabrics for our designs. In doing so, it's easy to underestimate the pizzazz we can add with our quilting threads. Here, the quiet of the solid fabrics provides a perfect canvas for our spiffy quilting. Bobbin-worked butterflies play peek-a-boo with the viewer, demanding a closer look. Made in solids to show off the quilting, wouldn't this quilt also be spectacular in batiks or tone-on-tone prints? Be still, my heart!

FINISHED SIZE: about 24½″ × 30½″   **PIECED, APPLIQUÉD, AND QUILTED**   quilted by Beth Ferrier, 2008

 ## materials

Yardage is based on 40″-wide fabric. Yardage amounts have been rounded up to include a little wiggle room. A fat quarter is 18″ × 22″. A fat eighth is 9″ × 22″.

- ⅞ yard of fabric for the background
- 1 fat quarter of fabric for the background accent and binding
- Assorted 5″ × 5″ charm squares of solid fabrics for the flower and leaf appliqués. (For my quilt, I grouped 4 charm squares—light, medium, dark, and center color—and made 1 each of the full flower, profile flower, and bud from that group.)
- 1 fat quarter or scraps of green fabric for the stem appliqués
- 1 fat quarter of medium gray fabric for the watering can appliqués
- 1 fat eighth each of dark gray and light gray for the watering can appliqués
- 29″ × 35″ rectangle (⅞ yard) of fabric for backing
- 29″ × 35″ piece of batting
- Water-soluble paper (two 5″ × 5″ squares) for the quilted bobbin-worked butterflies
- El Molino rayon thread from Presencia for the bobbin-work butterflies
- 2 yards of freezer paper

cutting

FROM THE BACKGROUND FABRIC

Cut 1 strip 12½″ × WOF. Cut into 1 rectangle 12½″ × 24½″, and label it "D." Trim the leftover strip to 11″ wide. Cut into 1 rectangle 16½″ × 11″, and label it "C."

Cut 1 strip 8″ × WOF. Cut into 1 rectangle 8″ × 24½″, and label it "A." Trim the leftover strip to 4½″ wide. Cut into 1 rectangle 4½″ × 11″ labeled "B" and 2 other rectangles 4½″ × 2″.

FROM THE BACKGROUND ACCENT FABRIC

Cut 6 strips 2″ × WOF (about 22″) for the binding.

Cut 3 rectangles 3″ × 4½″.

FROM THE STEM FABRIC

Cut a couple 1″ strips on the bias (see page 12) about a length of 12″ is all that's needed.

 ## make the background

Unless otherwise noted, all pieced seam allowances are ¼″. The background piecing in my quilt is super subtle. You can be a little more bold if you'd like.

1. Gather up the background accent fabric rectangles (3″ × 4½″) and the smallest background fabric rectangles (2″ × 4½″). Sew them together, matching the 4½″ edges. Press the seams toward the accent fabric rectangles.

Sew accent strip.

2. Sew Rectangles B and C to the accent strip. Press the seams toward the accent strip.

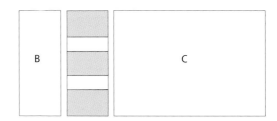

Add Rectangles B and C.

3. Add Rectangles A and D to the top and bottom. Press the seams toward the middle units. Ta-da! It's a background!

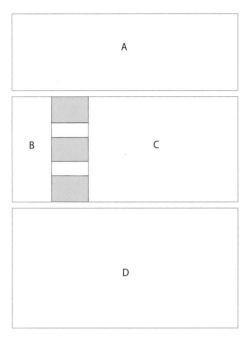

Add top and bottom rectangles.

1. Using the basic appliqué technique from Chapter One and the templates found on pages 78–79, create 6 flowers, 6 profile flowers, and 6 buds. Make bias stems following the directions on page 12. Then create 22 leaves and 1 watering can to hold it all.

2. Dock and stitch the pieces together. Stitch the appliqué motifs to the background using the project photo as a placement guide.

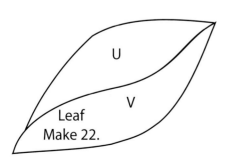

 finishing

The quilting is accomplished in three steps.

1. Stitch in the ditch around the appliqué shapes to provide a road map for placing the bobbin work.

2. Following the instructions on pages 34–37 and the template on page 70, pin the butterfly templates to the back of the quilt, and stitch them out with sexy bobbin thread.

3. All that is left is to quilt the background with your favorite fill pattern. Then bind and finish the quilt using your favorite method.

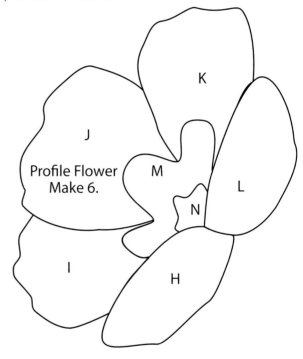

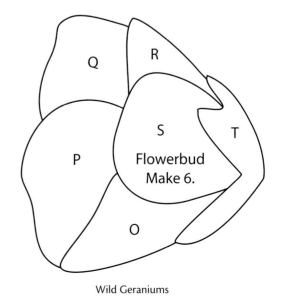

Wild Geraniums

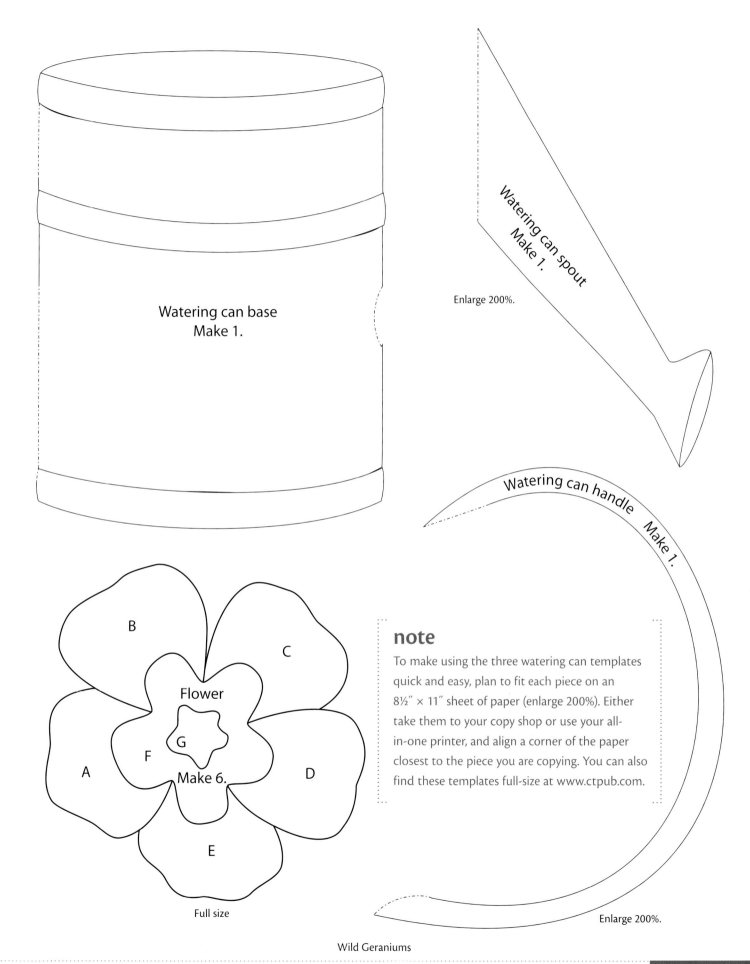

Watering can base
Make 1.

Watering can spout
Make 1.

Enlarge 200%.

Watering can handle   Make 1.

Enlarge 200%.

Flower

A
B
C
D
E
F
G

Make 6.

Full size

note

To make using the three watering can templates quick and easy, plan to fit each piece on an 8½″ × 11″ sheet of paper (enlarge 200%). Either take them to your copy shop or use your all-in-one printer, and align a corner of the paper closest to the piece you are copying. You can also find these templates full-size at www.ctpub.com.

Wild Geraniums

resources

We would be lost without our local quilt shops. Please check there first to find all the top-quality materials and tools that make quilting fun.

For those not blessed with a nearby shop:

SUPERIOR THREADS
www.superiorthreads.com

WONDERFIL THREADS
www.wonderfil.net

PRESENCIA
www.presenciausa.com

C&T WASH-AWAY APPLIQUÉ SHEETS
QUILTER'S FREEZER PAPER SHEETS
RICKY TIMS' EXTRA-WIDE FREEZER
PAPER
www.ctpub.com

EQUILTER.COM
This is a great online source for fabrics of all sorts.

about the author

A quilter since 1975, a teacher from the age of 17 months (when the first of five sisters was born), and a needle worker from the age of 5, Beth has had a lifelong love affair with needle and thread.

Beth describes her style as "rebellious traditional." Forever in search of easy and simply elegant solutions, Beth believes that when it comes to fabric, more is always better. Everything she designs is geared toward teaching skill-expanding tips and techniques.

Beth lives in Saginaw, Michigan, with her high school sweetheart, Kent, in a Greek Revival–style farmhouse that was built before 1860. Together they have four grown sons, one daughter-in-law (and a couple of girlfriends we hope to keep), and one precious grandson.

Great Titles *from* C&T PUBLISHING

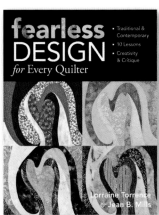

Available at your local retailer or **www.ctpub.com** *or* **800.284.1114**

For a list of other fine books from C&T Publishing, ask for a free catalog:

C&T PUBLISHING, INC.
P.O. Box 1456
Lafayette, CA 94549
(800) 284-1114

Email: ctinfo@ctpub.com
Website: www.ctpub.com

C&T Publishing's professional photography services are now available to the public. Visit us at www.ctmediaservices.com.

Tips and Techniques can be found at www.ctpub.com > Consumer Resources > Quiltmaking Basics: Tips & Techniques for Quiltmaking & More

For quilting supplies:

COTTON PATCH
1025 Brown Ave.
Lafayette, CA 94549
Store: (925) 284-1177
Mail order: (925) 283-7883

Email: CottonPa@aol.com
Website: www.quiltusa.com

Note: Fabrics used in the quilts shown may not be currently available, as fabric manufacturers keep most fabrics in print for only a short time.